Coldin
Eye

Chirnside

Duns

Polwarth

Greenlaw

Wark

R. Tweed

Norham

⊚ BERWICK UPON TWEED

Haggerston

Holy Island

Flodden

Wooler

Yetholm

Bamborough

Belford

Beadnell

Jedburgh

nam

Chillingham

Carter Bar

HEVIOT HILLS

Alnwick

Alwinton

Rothbury

Alnmouth

Warkworth

ielder

Otterburn

Cambo

Bellingham

Morpeth

padeadam

WALL

Corbridge

Hexham

R. Tyne

NEWCASTLE

Island

N

• *Blanchland*

→ *Direction of Route*

HO FOR THE BORDERS

HO FOR THE BORDERS

by
MICHAEL BRANDER

with photographs by
ALEX BROWN

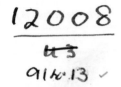

GEOFFREY BLES · LONDON

TEXT: © MICHAEL BRANDER, 1964
PHOTOGRAPHS: © ALEX BROWN, 1964

Printed in Great Britain
by Butler & Tanner Ltd., Frome and London
and published by
GEOFFREY BLES LTD.
52 DOUGHTY STREET, LONDON, W.C.1
33 YORK STREET, SYDNEY
531 LITTLE COLLINS STREET, MELBOURNE
47–53 CASTLEMAINE STREET, BRISBANE
CML BUILDING, KING WILLIAM STREET, ADELAIDE
WYNDHAM STREET, AUCKLAND
10 DYAS ROAD, DON MILLS, ONTARIO
P.O. BOX 8879, PALLSTATE HOUSE
51 COMMISSIONER STREET, JOHANNESBURG

First published 1964

To my mother
who was a Johnston

Acknowledgements

My thanks for their material help with this book are due, in order of route, to:

Mr. & Mrs. R. H. K. Hope
Mr. James Chisholm
Sir Eric de la Rue
Mr. & Mrs. Rankin Waddell
Mr. T. Laing.
Lt. Col. R. M. Ryan
Sir John Craster
The Rev. William Thompson
Mr. & Mrs. John B. Cormack
Mrs. F. T. Williams
The Duke of Buccleuch
Lt. Col. M. V. A. Wolfe-Murray
Lord Ferrier
Col. M. Crawford, and Mrs. Crawford of Dalgonar
The United Kingdom Atomic Energy Authority
The Earl and Countess of Carlisle
Messrs. Rolls Royce Ltd.
Mr. & Mrs. W. Sanderson
The Duke of Northumberland
Also to those who drove me round the route and have been
  labelled indiscriminately 'we'. Mr. E. T. Crisp, Mr. D.
  Green, Mr. R. H. Grose, Lt. Cdr. Brian Selby, R.N., Mr.
  G. C. Sterne
Also the librarian, Mr. T. W. Leslie, of East Lothian Library,
  and many other librarians in the Borders and elsewhere
And particularly to Alex Brown, Staff Photographer to the
  Scottish Tourist Board, for the illustrations.

Contents

Illustrations

ILLUSTRATIONS

MAP ON BOTH ENDPAPERS

xii

Introduction

THERE IS no other part of this country so fought over, so rich in history and legend, or so greatly renowned in verse and ballad as the Borders. A Borderer myself, on my mother's side, I realised how little I knew about the country between Hadrian's Wall and Berwick and I decided to learn more. In two previous books* I followed the routes taken by eighteenth-century travellers through parts of this country and compared their accounts with the present-day scene. In each case I was astonished how much I learned about a countryside which I thought I already knew reasonably well.

Each of these hunts (for hunts they became) was prefaced with the old hunting cry of 'Soho', used to encourage hounds on a scent. On this occasion, since I was concentrating on the countryside rather than on any one previous traveller's records, I dropped the title 'Soho', which in any case was liable to be confused with the area of London once known as Soho Fields, but now noted for veniality rather than venerie. I used instead the corruption of the same cry 'Ho', which was adopted by eighteenth- and nineteenth-century sportsmen when their pointers came on point at game.

Since comparisons with the eighteenth century had proved a sound means of learning about the countryside I decided to continue with this method, but promptly encountered a difficulty. It was not until the eighteenth century that settled agriculture had any chance to provide a permanent means of subsistence for the inhabitants of the Borders and even then their way of life was frequently miserable and poverty-stricken

* *Soho for the Colonel* (MacGibbon & Kee); *Soho for East Anglia* (Bles).

until improvements in farming had become generally accepted by the following century. Only a few intrepid travellers, such as Pennant, author of two famous *Scottish Tours* in the 1770s, and Colonel Thornton, author of *A Sporting Tour of the Highlands and Great Part of the North of England* in 1784, along with one or two others give an unbiased glimpse of life in parts of the Borders as it was before Sir Walter Scott cast his rose-coloured aura of romance over the Borders and Highlands alike.

Scarcely any two accounts of happenings in the Borders prior to 1800 seem to tally with each other and for my facts I have relied chiefly on the *Statistical Accounts* which were first compiled by the local clergy towards the end of the eighteenth century at the instance of Sir John Sinclair, and are one of the few reliable sources available. Otherwise it is largely a matter of personal choice as to which account seems most reliable just as it must be a matter of personal choice as to what area comprises the Borders.

The Romans made their most permanent border line at Hadrian's Wall, although they penetrated at times much further into Scotland. William the Conqueror extended his domain into Northumberland and the line of the Cheviots has remained roughly the Border ever since. To appreciate the Borders fully, however, it is necessary to explore both sides. Thus, parts of Northumberland, Cumberland, Dumfriesshire, Berwickshire and even Lanarkshire must be included as well as Roxburgh, Selkirk and Peebles. This is a vast area to cover intensively and no real attempt can be made to do so in a book limited to 224 pages. All that can be done is to look at some of the major points of interest and outstanding features of the past and the present in order to see the pattern as it is today.

To decide on a route was difficult. I travelled several thousand miles round the Borders before deciding on mine and even so found it impossible to cover all the places I wished to include. Berwick and the Merse seemed a sensible start. The sea coast of Northumberland and the Cheviot foothills seemed to follow logically. From there through to Liddesdale on the old reiver's route and thence up to the central Scottish mill towns was a natural progression. Through to the west and down to Hadrian's Wall was then the only route open and so back through Northumberland once more to the starting point. It is a route with more than enough of interest for several books. Of that I am well aware.

Since this was essentially a personal tour of discovery much has had to be left out that should have been included. In the circumstances that was inevitable, as I was not attempting to emulate Baedeker. It has been my aim to show as far as possible how the Borders have developed as they have and why the Borderers remain the sturdy individualists they are. In looking at the countryside and the people as they are today and as they have been in the past it is fascinating to realise that both are the products of over sixteen hundred years of battle, bloodshed and ballad.

Ho for the Borders. . . .

CHAPTER 1

Berwick to Polwarth

God send the land deliverance
Frae every reaving, riding Scot;
We'll sune hae neither cow nor ewe,
We'll sune hae neither staig nor stot.
"THE DEATH OF PARCY REED": BALLAD

Exact definition of the Borders defies geographic analysis, since over sixteen hundred years of battle, bloodshed and ballad are reflected not so much in physical boundaries as in the architecture and the character of the people themselves. Thus no two views on what area exactly comprises the Borders are likely to be precisely the same. It is a matter for personal choice, but perhaps the most obvious starting point is that most strikingly Border town of all, Berwick-upon-Tweed.

The last time I travelled from London to Scotland by train I was puzzled by the behaviour of a fellow passenger who left his seat promptly at each station and re-appeared panting slightly just as the train pulled out. In the course of conversation I learned that he came from Berwick and that his job took him away every week to various parts of the country. Eventually he explained his mysterious actions at each station.

"A railwayman friend of mine put me up to it," he confided. "You can save as much as thirty bob on a long journey by taking cheap day returns between each stop."

He went on to talk of Berwick.

"You'd think we were still living in the days of Jamie the One, instead of the twentieth century," he remarked of the

4

annual fair, which by ancient charter still blocks the Great North Road for a week in June each year. "But Berwick's a grand place to live in, mind."

The loyalty of those who live in Berwick towards their home town is understandable when one considers its unusual background. A walled town with a military tradition, a Border town, as well as a seaport at the mouth of a famous river, a county town divorced from its county, Berwick remains neither truly English or Scots. To appreciate why this is so it is necessary to glance briefly at its chequered history.

Famous once for its wool trade with Flanders, it was razed to the ground and its inhabitants massacred by Edward I. Between the twelfth and the fifteenth centuries it changed hands over a dozen times before finally being taken by Richard III, then Duke of Gloucester, in 1482. By treaty between Mary Queen of Scots and Edward VI it was later officially declared a 'free burgh' with its own government.

During the uncertain peace that followed, Elizabeth, on the earnest advice of her ministers, built a fortified wall round the town designed by an Italian, Portinari, on the latest European principles. It remains today the best example of its kind in Europe. Emphasis at that time was laid on the point that every Statute and Act of Parliament was applicable also "to our town of Berwick-upon-Tweed". By a civil service oversight, this continued for some hundreds of years until the Reform Act of 1885, when it was finally dropped, with the result that although Berwick declared war on Russia at the start of the Crimean War it has never officially made peace.

Although the Elizabethan walls were never tested, Berwick was still a garrison town as late as 1800 and in his *History of Berwick* of 1798, Dr. Fuller recorded:

The ancient practice of shutting the gates in garrison towns during the night, to the great annoyance not only of the inhabitants within the gates, but also to those in the suburbs, still prevails here. Physicians, surgeons and midwives are exempted, as well as those who come from them, but neither carriages, post-chaises, horses or carts are allowed to pass through them while shut. . . . [He added bitterly:] If a person on his first coming up to the gate, quarrels with the guard, the greatest importunities afterwards for admission will not be of any avail . . . even medical gentlemen returning from the country and though exhausted with fatigue and want of sleep, are sometimes detained there.

Yet it is chiefly due to the wall that Berwick retains the higgledy-piggledy appearance which is one of its chief attractions. Although most of the houses have been rebuilt or refaced since Elizabethan days there are many dating from the seventeenth and eighteenth centuries and the resulting hotch-potch of architectural styles, all shapes and sizes, red-tiled and slate-roofed, large and small side by side, makes an interesting and pleasing contrast to so many modern hen-coop model towns. The steep, curving, cobbled streets, the narrow wynds and the walls themselves above the tidal waters of the Tweed provide a peaceful picture today.

Long gone are the days of Berwick's commercial glory prior to the reign of Edward I, when it even rivalled London as a centre of trade. In 1776 Pennant wrote:

Abundance of wool is exported from this town; eggs in vast abundance collected through all the country, almost as far as Carlisle; they are packed up in boxes with the thick end downwards and are sent to London for the use of sugar refiners. The salmon fisheries here are very considerable and likewise bring in vast sums.

In the *Statistical Account* of 1792 one observer wrote:

The Tweed produces a great quantity of salmon, gilses and whitling trout, the last of which are carried alive in wells, in the Berwick smacks and weigh generally about 3 lbs. . . . One salmon in January 1791, not two stone in weight, sold for £3. 0s. 2d. at Berwick for the London market.

Today the salmon fisheries and the weekly market are about all that remain of Berwick's former extensive commerce. It is notable, however, that the Berwick Salmon Fisheries Ltd. are an extremely efficiently run and successful public company. I visited their offices at the river's edge below the Elizabethan Wall and Mr. Reed, director and secretary, explained how they still worked on the old net and coble principle. They employ around a hundred men in the season and most of them have regular part-time agricultural work during the off-season. With a wages bill of around £10,000 a year the company still managed to pay a regular dividend of over 20 per cent annually. It is said that a healthy netting industry makes a healthy river and in the case of the Tweed this would seem to be true. Probably the town itself benefits more from the fisheries than might at once be apparent, for there are almost certainly a considerable number of small shareholders living in Berwick.

In spite of the barracks, which, until the decision to vacate them was made in 1963, were the oldest occupied barracks in the country, Berwick does not give the impression of being a military town. It is a county town outside its county yet remaining a county centre with a certain mellow charm and dignity. It has something of the dreaming air of a university town and if a site for a new university in the Borders was required it would be hard to find a more suitable choice.

The town hall in the centre of the High Street is a notable building, erected between 1754 and 1761. Dr. Fuller noted: "It is a stately pile of modern architecture, consisting of finely hewn stone, three stories high, a handsome spire and a beautiful pediment, supported by four graceful columns of the Tuscan order." A subsequent historian of the town added: "It has been remarked that the building bears some resemblance to an inverted mustard pot with a vinegar cruet on top."

Surprisingly enough, the top floor was used as a gaol. Dr. Fuller wrote:

The upper flat is occupied as a common gaol, and is perhaps

7

the most healthy and pleasant one in the kingdom. This is owing to its many large windows, from which the prisoners enjoy several excellent views of the Town, the German Ocean, Bambro' Castle and Holy Island. There is a long gallery which they are allowed to perambulate. Tradesmen when confined have a liberty to work in this gaol. We have even heard of some who retrieved their fortunes in it.

Persons laid up for debt or petty offences are permitted to walk on the roof of the building to enjoy the free air. This circumstance together with the extensive and beautiful surrounding prospects already noticed, must be both a pleasant and salutary indulgence to the prisoners.

It was not until nearly halfway through the nineteenth century that the top floor of the town hall ceased to be used for this purpose. A historian noted, not surprisingly:

One prisoner, during his occupation of picking oakum, abstracted as much as made him a rude rope, which he twisted himself; and stealing to the balustrades on the roof, he affixed his frail line and fearlessly lowered himself down. The rope parted when he was halfway, and he fell on a butcher's stall, that broke his fall, and got safely off.

The castle, which withstood the assaults of Edward III and his forces massed on Halidon Hill above the town, was finally levelled to make way for the railway station in 1850. Where the main line trains halt, Edward I crowned Balliol King of Scots in 1291. Although the town is now part of England and subject to English law, the county which bears its name remains still a part of Scotland. Yet, though Berwick, as part of Northumberland, shares an English M.P., its football team plays in the Scottish League. Such anachronisms abound in this town, which is neither wholly English nor Scots, but an amalgam of the two.

Although Berwick's embattled past is long forgotten, it is amusing to recall the last time the streets echoed with the sound of soldiery called to arms. On the 1st of February 1804, the countryside was standing to in imminent fear of Napoleonic invasion when the sentry on Halidon Hill suddenly saw the warning beacon on Duns Law ablaze. Other beacons inland were soon alight and after a slight, if understandable, hesitation, he too applied his torch to the signal bonfire on the heights. In a few minutes the call to arms was sounding in the town and the drums beating their feverish alarm tattoo.

In a surprisingly short space of time the Yeomanry of Berwickshire, gentlemen riders all, under the command of Colonel Buchan of Kelso, came thundering through the cobbled streets on their high-bred horses.

Riding at a sharp trot over the Bridge, with their accoutrements ringing and clashing with their speed, came the Haggerston troop, commanded by its Colonel, Sir Carnaby Haggerstone. The Eyemouth Militia dashed hurriedly along at double quick time . . . the Chirnside Volunteers, the Hutton Trainbands, the soldiers of Ladykirk and the tenantry of Ford and Tilmouth Castle headed by their respective landlords. . . .

A brave sight they must have made. Unfortunately it all turned out to be the 'Great False Alarm'. In the morning, when the news finally came through, they dispersed again, no doubt much relieved.

Three miles to the north of Berwick is Lamberton Toll, the point marking the border between England and Scotland. Here the Scottish Tourist Board have erected a sign 'Welcome to Scotland', where in the past many eloping couples must have been eagerly awaiting to tie the knot. The Lamberton tollkeeper, whose reputation at one time vied with that of the smith at Gretna Green and the bridge-keeper at Coldstream, no longer levies his toll although his toll house still stands by the roadside. Those who marry in haste to repent at leisure may not appreciate the other side of the Scottish Tourist Board sign, which reads: 'Haste Ye Back'.

It is probably not generally realised that as late as 1923 a girl over twelve and a boy over fourteen could be legally married in Scotland simply by declaration, without any question of parental consent. It was not until 1940 that marriage by declaration was made illegal, but even so marriage in Scotland is still easier for minors than anywhere on the Continent. The only qualifications required by Scottish law are that the couple must be over sixteen and have been resident in the country for twenty-five days.

The actual procedure is simplicity itself. After fifteen clear days residence in the country, the sixteen-year-old couple may enter notice of marriage for a fee of one shilling paid to the local Registrar. They may at the same time buy a certificate of marriage for one and sixpence. After a further seven clear days they must appear before the Registrar with two witnesses over sixteen and accept each other as man and wife. The marriage certificate is duly registered and they pay a further five shillings: Total cost seven and sixpence, the same as a dog licence.

The romantic Scot returning across the Border after any length of time has been known to sniff the air appreciatively and murmur: "How much better the air smells this side of the Border." The romance of the Border has even been known to affect such hardened cynics as antique dealers, whose every dealing is a matter of romance, if they care to view it so. The story runs that not so long ago a certain Scottish antique dealer returning from the London sale rooms had with him in his car a part of Prince Charles's camp kit, which had been captured at Culloden and ever since had been outside Scotland. As he neared the Border the thought came to him that this was an exceptional, almost a historic, occasion. Finally as he approached the boundary line he drew to a halt. Going to the boot of the car he unwrapped the cherished object and marched solemnly over the Border carrying it ceremoniously in front of him.

My East Anglian farming friend and I drove on to Eyemouth, where I had heard that the sight to see was the lobster ponds during the months from July to September. It was with some difficulty that we found them, in a yard off the quayside, for at first sight they look more like two rows of oblong concrete pig pens with a passage down the centre, rather than the ponds we had expected. A constant gushing of salt water from pipes in the walls at the far end of the shed in which they are housed inhibits conversation. It was only on entering the passageway that we realised that each pen was filled with hundreds of lobsters neatly graded for size from 1½-pounders to 4-pounders, their claws bound with elastic bands, all swimming, or crawling, ceaselessly round their watery prisons.

"Where do they all come from?" I asked.

"All over Scotland, as far as Stornoway."

"How many are there in there now?"

"About ten thousand."

"Where do they all go to?"

"There are five thousand away to France tomorrow."

"By air, I suppose?"

"Aye, by air. They're packed in special light cardboard cases."

"By train they would travel in ordinary fish boxes, would they?"

"Aye. Packed in sawdust to stop them getting damaged."

"Do you damp the sawdust?"

"No. Leave it dry. That way they last the journey all right."

I gave up trying to compete against the steady roar of rushing water, but I was reminded of the "eggs in vast abundance collected through all the country" and the "whitling trout carried to London alive in wells in the Berwick smacks". I did not enquire the current market price, but I remembered Dr. Fuller's indignant note: "Some years ago a good lobster might have been purchased for 3*d.*, now 6*d.* and 8*d.* are given for them."

As I walked up and down the narrow passageway between the ponds filled with milling mottled purple life, I meditated on the unlikely thought that in a couple of days these same lobsters would probably be gracing the gourmets' tables in various Paris restaurants. One of them might even end up on the table of some friends of mine I knew to be there. Grouse I could understand being flown to France, but in my innocence I had imagined that they had a plentiful supply of shellfish of their own. It scarcely seemed worth while going to France for such delicacies when they could be obtained a good deal fresher on the spot. Yet as I looked around me once again I felt the desire to eat lobster leaving me rapidly. A cooked lobster on a plate is one thing, but ten thousand live ones all around is quite another.

We went on to explore Eyemouth. It is essentially a fishing port and with the harbour alterations at present taking place, it is likely to become one of the most important on the east coast. Already the modern school there produces a higher percentage of passes in navigation than any other school in Scotland. With a complete ship's bridge and accessories available for study this is perhaps not surprising, but seamanship must be in the blood of the youngsters born here.

It is perhaps as well that one other erstwhile dominant Eyemouth characteristic has not been passed on, for at one time after the Union of 1707, when cheating the revenue men was regarded as natural and even necessary, the town was the centre of considerable smuggling traffic. In 1792, however, in the *Statistical Account*, the Rev. George Tod was able to write:

For several years past, there has not been a single smuggler residing in this parish. The former dealers in that illicit trade are now all dead, or removed to distant parts. Not one of them died rich; and the far the greatest part of them became bankrupt.

At that time Eyemouth was so full of hiding places for smuggled goods that it was sometimes said there was as much of the town below ground as there was above. Gunsgreen House, which overlooks the harbour mouth, was, so we learned, full of secret passages. We went over to look at it, but soon gathered that it had been reduced to the status of a boarding house and was full of guests, for one of Eyemouth's flourishing secondary industries today is the holiday trade, which goes with almost every seaside town.

"Aye, there's a fireplace which used to swing back and there's a secret passage behind it," we were told. "But we blocked it up because of the draughts and you can't see the house just now because we can't disturb our guests."

Our informant, the son of the present owner, is a policeman. In itself one feels this is enough to make some former bankrupted owner rise in his grave to disturb the sleep of the paying guests with muffled noises in the secret passages. It is a handsome enough house, though now sadly dilapidated, both inside and out, as we found when the owner relented and agreed to show us round, leading us from room to room filled with beds of every shape and size. Without electricity or modern plumbing, running such a guest house must have been a formidable task and it was no surprise to learn that this was to be the final year.

Clearly once a smuggling centre of note, since it has such unusual attributes as a tea shute lined with zinc running from cellar to attic and an underground entrance from the harbour, this house merits preservation before it is too late. Facing it across the harbour the old part of Eyemouth is an attractive small town centring naturally on the life around the quays where the fish markets are held on the return of the fishing fleet.

This is a part of the countryside where the Berwickshire wit and pungent character are savoured at their saltiest. Driving towards Coldingham in thick east coast haar, or mist, I recounted a couple of stories to my East Anglian farming friend by way of explaining the Berwickshire character. One concerned a local worthy known far and wide as 'Jockie' Johnson. Driving his fish cart with his pony in the shafts 'Jockie' was a well-known figure in the countryside. One day the hounds of the Berwickshire hunt passed him on the moors in full cry after a fox. At once Jockie rose in his seat and standing braced like a charioteer whipped his pony into a gallop. Haddocks, herrings and fish boxes flew out behind him as the cart rocked from side to side, but Jockie paid no heed, merely encouraging his pony to greater efforts.

"What are ye aboot, Jockie?" demanded the huntsman in amazement, as he drew level with him. "Ye're losing a' yer fish, man."

"To hell wi' the fish," retorted Jockie, plying his whip harder than ever. "We maun keep up wi' the gentry."

Another famous character of whom I had been told was one 'Tarbrush', so called, I was informed, because in the days when every fisherman tarred his boat the subject arose of raising £20 to paint the church at St. Abbs and he was heard to burst forth:

"Twenty punds to paint the kirk. What's wrong wi' a tarbrush? Tar the b . . ."

My friend was too busy driving to pay much attention.

"Hardly the weather for writing travel books when you can't even see the hedges on either side of the road," he grumbled.

"It's surprising how things turn up quite unexpectedly, just the same," I encouraged him.

Fortunately it was not long before we drew into Coldingham. It was our intention to visit the church there, but before doing so, by mutual consent, we turned into the comfortable little inn. In one corner in a blue jersey and peaked cap sat an ancient bearded mariner with a hypnotic twinkling eye deep in conversation with another obviously local man. A brief conversation about the weather followed and so broad were the Berwickshire accents that I found myself literally having to translate for the benefit of my friend.

"Let's go and see that church," he said, finishing his drink. "I'm beginning to feel like a foreigner in here."

As we turned to go I noticed a self-effacing youth enter and

14

start to say something to the elderly mariner and his friend about 'witnesses', but paying no further attention I followed my friend into the mist outside.

It was definitely not the weather for lingering in graveyards or amid the doubtful pleasures of damp ruins, however impressive they might be in the sunlight. We could still see enough to appreciate that Coldingham Priory must once have been a most impressive foundation and the reason for the growth of Coldingham as a village. Like so many other monasteries it was sacked at the time of the Reformation and the ruins used as a quarry for the surrounding countryside.

The red sandstone arch, all that is left of the outside of the old priory church, loomed gauntly above our heads as we approached the modern church. Incorporating part of the old choir, this is certainly an impressive local kirk. With the mist curling in twisting coils around them, the highly varnished pews seemed a little incongruous against the ancient background of carved stone. Even so and even in such conditions enough remains to visualise something of the splendour which must have been Coldingham Priory Church before the Reformation.

We returned with mutual accord for further 'refreshment' and found a scene of celebration at the inn.

"We've just had a runaway wedding," announced the landlady dramatically, "Brush, here, was a witness."

Now shortened by sixty years' familiar use from 'Tarbrush' to 'Brush' it transpired that the elderly mariner was none other than 'Captain' Johnson, the famous 'Tarbrush' himself (see pl. 1). The self-effacing youth I had noticed had been one half of a runaway couple of teenagers from Huddersfield. According to 'Tarbrush' the bridegroom's epic first words after signing the register were:

"Well, we've done it at last."

In the circumstances it was rather longer than we had anticipated before we continued on our journey, but fortunately by then the mist had begun to lift and, as we struck inland, more of the countryside became visible. Even so it was extremely difficult to read a map accurately and we missed the turning to Linthill House a mile or two away, where a notorious murder took place. 'Tarbrush' assured us that he remembered seeing bloodstained panelling removed from the house when he was a boy. As the murder took place in 1752 this proves either the power of local legend or the atrocious bloodiness of the deed.

Old Mrs. Hume, the owner of the house at that time, had a strongbox full of gold in her bedroom. The door was locked by a simple though ingenious bolt, which fell into place by its own weight, but which could be lifted by a pulley arrangement from her bed when required. Her trusted butler, Norman Ross by name, overcome by greed, blocked the bolt-hole with cherry stones and in the dark hours crept into her room to break open the strongbox. Wakened by his attempts to find the key, the old lady, with the courage common to most elderly Scots ladies, grappled with him, whereupon in a fit of sudden frenzy he slit her throat from ear to ear. Leaving her for dead on the floor, he continued his search for the key; but the old lady was not done for yet. Hearing a noise behind him, he was horrified to see a ghastly bloody figure groping blindly for the bell rope. Before he could stop her, the warning bell rang out and he was trapped in her bed-chamber with blood everywhere and her corpse at his feet. In a fit of panic he leaped from the window, breaking his leg as he landed. Found some days later, hiding in some bushes nearby, he was the last man in Scotland to be hung in chains, having been caught 'red-handed' with his victim's blood still visible on him. Towards the turn of the century the bloodstained imprints of his victim's hands were said to be still clearly visible on the panelling of the room where the murder took place, just as 'Tarbrush' remembered.

After losing our way amidst a maze of side roads a signpost

caught my eye, marked simply 'Edin's Hall Broch'. We turned down a rocky side road and arrived amongst a number of parked cars above the Whiteadder. After a walk of twenty minutes or so past a gamekeeper's cottage and across some stony fields we came to the Broch. An ancient pre-Pictish fortress, what is left of it seems in a surprisingly good state of repair. This is probably due largely to the Ministry of Works, for according to the *Statistical Account* of 1840 it was being used indiscriminately as a quarry in those days and was in danger of disappearing altogether.

Circular, some forty to fifty feet across, the dry stone walls are twelve to fifteen feet thick and about five feet is still left standing, consisting of interlocked whinstones, often of considerable size. No mortar is used anywhere. Four separate cells are enclosed in the walls. Compared with, for instance, the Broch of Mousa in the Shetland Islands, or even the Broch at Strathmore, there is very little left of this, but it is still amongst the best of its kind in the Borders area. To imagine the walls thirty feet higher requires quite an imagination, but as a sample of how prehistoric man existed in these lonely hills it is worth the walk.

On the way back we stopped for a chat with the gamekeeper and enquired whether he found visitors to the encampment a nuisance to his birds.

"Oh, aye, they're a pest," he confessed. "They're aye tramp, trampin' about the place, treading on nests and letting their dogs roam about or leaving the gates open and the like."

It must be difficult for farmers and gamekeepers who have such monuments of public interest on their land, for inevitably there are some visitors either too ignorant, or too careless, to pay attention to the elementary decencies of life in the country. It may be hard for the townsman accustomed to exercising his dog in the public parks to realise that allowing it to run free where there are ewes in lamb, or sitting birds during the nesting season, simply cannot be tolerated. Yet today sufficient people can and do visit the countryside for them to learn the elementary codes of behaviour.

We returned to the car and soon afterwards, on asking our way to Broomhouse, were gratuitously informed that we had just passed the Chirnside farm of sheep farmer Jim Clark, who is also world champion racing driver. We were in search of the grave of a man who had been fast on a horse, although, un-fortunately for him, not quite fast enough. Broomhouse is the site of the grave of Sir Anthony Darcy, le Sieur de Beauté, but since a nineteenth-century roadmender used the cairn which marked the spot as a convenient source of road metal 'Bawtie's Grave' can no longer be traced.

Darcy was appointed Warden of the East and Middle Marches of the Merse and Teviotdale in 1516 after, it was said, having taken part in the treacherous execution of Lord Alexander Home, the previous Warden, and his brother. The Homes planned vengeance and in 1517 Sir David Home, with a picked band of followers, encountered the new Warden with a small party of equal numbers south of Duns. A quarrel was picked and the Warden's party was attacked. He was forced to ride for his life. At Broomhouse his horse was bogged. He was caught. His head was promptly hacked off and flaunted in triumph, some say on the battlements of Hume Castle, others on the Market Cross in Duns. The Homes, like most Borderers, were not ones to forgive easily.

Writing on Duns in 1791, the Rev. Dr. Robert Bowmaker recorded in the *Statistical Account*:

Berwickshire is nominally divided into three districts, the Merse, Lammermoor and Lauderdale. The Merse is that flat part of the county which is bounded by the River Tweed on the south and south-east; by part of Tiviotdale and Lauderdale on the south-west and west and by the Lammermoor hills on the north-west and north, with the town of Berwick at the east point. It is a plain of at least 25 miles from east to west and 15 from north to south and takes the name of Merse (or March) from being a border county. At the head of this plain and in the very centre of the county stands the town of Dunse, encompassed on the west, north and east, by the Lammermoor hills.

After this preamble the Rev. Bowmaker seems to have been hard pushed to find much to say about Duns. He mentioned the fact that it had been briefly popular as a spa in the mid-eighteenth century. Under the heading 'Miscellaneous' he noted:

On the 18th September 1790 was found, three miles south-east from Dunse, a bird very rare in Scotland. It was killed by a cat and discovered to be the bird called Hoopoe by the English, the Upupa of the Ancients.

He also mentioned, under the title 'Learned Men': "The celebrated metaphysician and theologist John Duns Scotus was born in Dunse in 1274." Whereas few people will have heard of John Duns Scotus today an entry in the *Gazetteer* of 1832 gives further details:

It is a common story that the word *dunce* was derived from this scholar's local appelation, being applied by way of irony to stupid scholars on the same principle as a heavy fellow is play-fully styled a *bright man*.

Duns, the county town of Berwickshire since 1903, with the aggressive motto "Duns Dings A' ", is almost aggressively Scots in appearance. Its market square is surrounded by a jumble of grey stone upright houses of varying shape and size. We drove through to the home of Sir Eric de la Rue at Caldra. Here he demonstrated his Caldra method of catching rabbits. Sir Eric, besides being an excellent shot and all-round sports-man, belongs to that enthusiastic minority of inventors who refuse to give up until they have achieved as near perfection as possible. On leaving the army after the war, he decided to try to find the answer to the rabbits then abounding everywhere. Starting with the idea that long netting was the answer, he set about trying to improve on the age-old method of using nets of forty yards or so long.

"I started off with two nets," he explained. "Then I decided that wasn't enough, so then I tried three together."

Finding that this did not provide the answer he tried again with four, then five. Time and again he found his theories failed to work in practice and required modification. Slowly his invention began to take shape. Finally, ten years after he had started, he had achieved near-perfection. Wheeling a balloon-tyred barrow carrying nearly a mile of long nets in rolls un-winding behind him, he was able to surround whole fields with netting silently and quickly with the aid of only one assistant to stake the nets behind him. Thereafter it was merely a matter of driving the rabbits into the nets and very considerable bags could be made in this way.

Unfortunately it was at this stage, when his invention might have achieved considerable fame, that myxomatosis spread throughout the country. For the past ten years the prototype has been mouldering in a shed unused but, meanwhile, the rabbits, with their phenomenal ability to survive, have been returning throughout the country, in spite of rabbit clearance societies and gassing. As the most efficient method I have seen of dealing with those rabbits in otherwise inaccessible places, it seems to me that nearly twenty years after he first started experimenting Sir Eric's invention might well come into its own at last. For anyone interested in keeping down rabbits effectively and cheaply it merits investigation.

Not far beyond Caldra, above the Blackadder, is Polwarth. As we drove towards the church there I asked my friend what he thought of the countryside he had seen.

"I have to admit that anywhere that can produce a world champion racing driver and a prime minister, as well as some of the people we've met, must have something,' he declared. "Anyway it's a good start."

1. "An ancient bearded mariner with a hypnotic twinkling eye."
"Tarbrush" Johnson (p. 14)

2. "As obscure as the Eton Wall Game." Handball in Duns (p. 114)

"An impressive local kirk." Coldingham Priory from a print *c.* 1830 (p. 15)

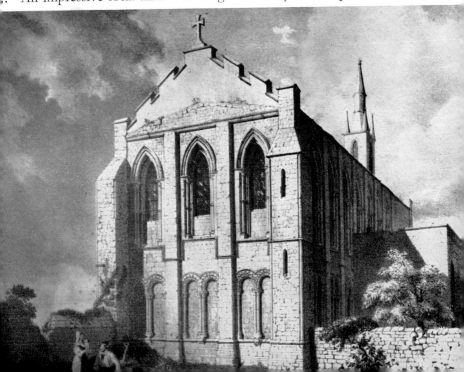

CHAPTER 2

Polwarth to Kelso

The lasses o' Lauder are mim and meek,
The lasses o' the Fanns smell o' peat reek,
The lasses o' Gordon canna sew a steek,
But weel can they sup their crowdie!
The lasses o' Earlston are bonnie and braw,
The lasses o' Greenlaw are black as a craw,
But the lasses o' Polwart are the best o' them a'.

TRADITIONAL VERSE

POLWARTH CHURCH, with its attractive tower and belfry, bears a strange resemblance from a distance to a child's toy church built of bricks (see pl. 4). It has the same stark simplicity of line and the tower and belfry look strangely like an afterthought. This is not at all surprising once one knows the history of the church (which is reputed to have been built originally in A.D. 900), because the tower was indeed a later addition. It and the belfry were added by the Polwarth family in 1703, after their return from exile in Holland, and thereby hangs a tale:

In 1685 Sir Patrick Hume of Polwarth was indicted by King James II for plotting rebellion. Warning came in advance of the troopers sent to arrest him, via a trusted tradesman. The problem was to find a secure hiding place in a matter of minutes. Tradition has it that his young daughter, Lady Mary Grizell, aged twelve, was the first to think of hiding in the vault beneath Polwarth Church There, for a month, Sir Patrick lay hidden, fed clandestinely by his intrepid daughter under cover of darkness each night.

Finally, fearing that the vault was no longer safe, another hiding place was prepared in the cellars of the house, but was found to fill with water. As they were wondering what to do warning of another search came in the form of a single feather sent by a neighbour ahead of the troopers engaged on it. It was the traditional signal to take flight and Sir Patrick took the hint. He fled to London disguised and thence to the Continent. There his family joined him, and after four years of privation with them, he returned in triumph as Earl of Marchmont and Polwarth with King William of Orange in 1688.

The vault beneath the church still exists and a dark and gloomy hiding place it must have been. Closed in the seventeenth century by a stone, it now has bars across the entrance. It now contains four lead coffins of the Polwarth family. On the apex of the east gable, above the entrance to the vault, is an orange surmounted by a crown, representing the House of Orange.

In common with most Scots churches it was locked and we felt it would be interesting to look over it if possible. Lying in full view across a stretch of meadow, about half a mile away, was an attractive late-eighteenth-century porticoed and bow-fronted house, which we decided must obviously be the manse. We drove up to it and I rang the bell. In spite of the prevalent fashion for ministers not to wear obviously ministerial garb I felt instinctively that the grey-haired dark-moustached gentleman in checked tweeds who opened the door could not be the minister.

"I wondered if you would happen to have the key of the church?" I asked. "I thought this was probably the manse, but I suspect this is one of those divided parishes where the minister lives elsewhere and covers two parishes."

This approach was greeted with a broad smile.

"It so happens that I drive a vintage Bentley, which I race at Charterhall," was the reply. "And when we first moved in here someone was heard to say to one of the locals, 'My, that's surely a very sporting new minister you've got, I saw him racing at Charterhall the other day.' "

I countered by replying that I normally drove a 1926 Rolls Royce, which happened at that moment to be undergoing repairs. From this one thing led to another, including a discussion on the architecture of the manse and advice on what to look for in the church. It was obvious that Mr. Bennett, for it transpired that that was his name, was a keen antiquarian, with a considerable knowledge of history and wide interests. I asked him whether he farmed.

"No, I'm an antique dealer," he replied.

It struck me that Polwarth was hardly the sort of centre one normally finds antique dealers and I suggested as much discreetly, enquiring his particular interests.

"Oh, I buy and sell internationally," he explained, with a wave of his hand. "I'm a horologist."

From that the discussion passed to shooting and labradors, for he had a useful-looking black dog on his doorstep behind him. Finally, drawing our attention to the similarity of the tower to a Dutch tower, especially in the matter of the roof beams, which he referred to as 'a bat's nest', he handed over the key.

On our way back to the church my friend, more versed in horological matters than I, assured me that he had read horological papers and articles by G. W. Bennett, and that his name was well known internationally. I was content to have enjoyed my conversation with him and also to have obtained the key of the church. In practice the interior proved full of interest.

Amongst various curiosities in the church were a pair of old 'Kirk Ladles' for the collection, reminding me irresistibly of a pair of croupier's rakes. Beside them was the 'Morton Deid Bell' used as late as 1715 to frighten away evil spirits in the front of the coffin on the way to the grave. Perhaps the most striking feature of the church, however, is the 'Laird's Bole Hole' in the tower. This was a particularly convenient arrangement consisting of a small opening with a sliding shutter from a room in the tower looking down on to the altar, above the heads of the congregation. Thus the laird could sit in comfort and listen to the service, or not, as he wished. He also had a hidden means of exit, if he wanted it. The Polwarth family certainly built the tower with an eye to their own convenience.

We returned the key of the church to Mr. Bennett the sporting horologist and drove on to Greenlaw, across a sweeping stretch of moorland. The overnight coaches to London still halt in Greenlaw as their horse-drawn predecessors did in more leisurely days. For a similar all too brief halt the passengers adjourn for a hurried cup of tea or a drink in the bar of the old coaching inn, the Castle. Opposite the inn, the village green is dominated by what at first appears to be a surprisingly large and imposing town hall with Corinthian pillars and Byzantine dome. For such a small place it seems somewhat out of proportion but we learned that this was a relic of the days between 1696 and 1853 when Greenlaw was the county town of Berwickshire. This was then the County Buildings, where the Sheriff Court was held.

Greenlaw itself dates only from the end of the seventeenth century, when it was moved from an older site, and from this period dates the church with what seems to be its large tower. Prior to the erection of the County Buildings on the green, this tower was in fact the old Tolbooth, or prison. On the west side, opposite to the church, then stood the old county court. This gave rise to the jingle:

> Here stands the Gospel and the Law
> Wi' Hell's Hole atwixt the twa.

After some difficulty in locating the beadle and obtaining the key we managed to penetrate 'Hell's Hole'. It is a massively built tower with an unusual square newel stair and grim reminders of past prisoners still survive in the form of various barely decipherable graffiti on the walls. It must unquestionably have seemed a 'Hell's Hole' indeed to those unlucky enough to have been imprisoned there inside those immensely thick walls. Merely to step through the door into the dark interior is to experience an immediate sense of claustrophobia.

The last man publicly hanged in the county was buried under the prison in 1834. Ironically enough, much of the upper space where the prisoners did their time is now filled with the works of the clock which today graces the tower with its three faces overlooking the town. In spite of its grim history, the old Tolbooth continues to perform a useful and even decorative function.

In the churchyard I was impressed by the tombstone in memory of James Johnson, Governor of Greenlaw prison, who died in 1800. Not only he but his wife and his considerable family and descendants, both before and after that date, as late as the 1930s, are also commemorated on the same stone. The list of those who died in infancy makes one appreciate the advantages of modern hygiene and its effect on infant mortality. As both sides of the stone are now nearly filled any further descendants wishing to add their names are liable to be disappointed.

Not far beyond Greenlaw on the Lauder road is a farm owned by Mr. Rankin Waddell to whom, some years ago, I had sold a young gundog bitch. It says much for the bitch and for him that we have been friends ever since and I have followed his successes in field trials and shows with natural interest and approval. His farm has the strange name of Rumbleton and checking the old spelling of this I found that in the seventeenth century it was written as Rummeltoun. It is in fact a corruption of Roman Town, or Roman Camp, for here the Romans once had an outpost and on nearby Rumbleton Law a Roman camp was once sited. Waiting nearby for duck at flighting time with the wind soughing over the fields and stone dykes, listening to the whicker of wings overhead, it was possible to imagine the Roman legionaries far from their native

Rome hearing the same haunting sounds in the same evening twilight.

Further on the road to Lauder is the estate of Spottiswoode, owned in the nineteenth century by Lord John Scott, whose wife wrote the words and music for *Annie Laurie*, amongst the best known of all Scottish songs. Although the house is now demolished there is a reminder of the old coaching days in the shape of two lodges still standing by the roadside, the quaint conceit of the laird. Pseudo-Gothic, they record on milestones set in the walls the distances to the major coaching points between London and Edinburgh. Two stone clock faces, one above each lodge, stand permanently at the times at which the coaches were due from north and south.

On seeing these, a scientist friend who was with me, was at once reminded of the computer which was fed the apparently simple problem of whether it was preferable to have a watch which was ten minutes slow, or one that had stopped altogether. Surprisingly, the machine opted for the one that had stopped on the grounds that it was at least right once every twelve hours whereas the other never was. By those standards the laird of Spottiswoode has the last laugh.

Approaching Lauder from this direction, one sees first the gates of Thirlestane Castle. Pennant's description of this in 1775 was: "a singular old house of the earl of Lauderdale. The front small, bounded on each side with a great round tower, capt with slated cones." It is obvious at a glance that the front of the house was added to in the nineteenth century, based as it was on an old fortified tower of tremendous strength, but already by Pennant's day the transformation from a fort to a mansion house had taken place.

Arriving to see the house by appointment, I found myself unexpectedly involved with two bus-loads of chartered accountants and their wives sightseeing in the intervals of a World Convention of their profession held in Edinburgh. Amidst a minor babel of languages, we were led round the

26

main rooms of the castle by the elderly butler, Lawrence. To my delight, he retold the story of Midside Maggie, which to my mind is the best one connected with the Lauderdales and has the virtue of being entirely true.

Midside Maggie was the young wife of Thomas Hardie, tenant of Tollishill, one of the Lauderdale farms in the seventeenth century. One severe winter, they lost many sheep and it became obvious that they would be unable to pay the rent due. She went to the laird, who was not a man of pleasing character, and begged to be excused the rent on this occasion. He replied shortly and, as he no doubt thought, conclusively:

"Bring me the rent due in June, or a snowball."

Not a whit discomfited, Maggie retired to the hills where she rolled a monster snowball into a deep, well-sheltered cleft which seldom saw the sun. Thus, in June, to the laird's obvious surprise, she was able to produce the snowball he had scoffingly demanded in lieu of rent.

To do him justice, he did not go back on his word and the Hardies retained their farm. Then came the Civil War and the Commonwealth and as a staunch Royalist he was imprisoned in the Tower of London. For a number of years no rent was paid by any of the Lauderdale tenants, but, in spite of their prosperity, Midside Maggie felt her conscience uneasy at the memory of what she considered to be the laird's kindness to her husband and herself.

Eventually she insisted on baking the rent due in gold coins into a large bannock and, with this concealed in a plaid, and escorted by her husband, she made the long journey to London on foot. Once there she obtained permission to see the prisoner and presented him with the golden bannock. With the money he purchased his release to the Continent and, returning soon afterwards in triumph with Charles II, one of his first actions was to grant Midside Maggie and her heirs the lease of the farm in perpetuity. He also presented her with a magnificent silver stomacher, which is now to be seen in the Scottish

National Museum of Antiquities in Edinburgh. In passing, it is of interest to note that the last descendant of Midside Maggie of Tollishill emigrated to Canada in the '30s of this century.

Pennant also noted of Thirlestane Castle:

The inside had been heavily stuccoed by the Duke of Lauderdale, one of the noted Cabal in the time of Charles II. His portrait by Lely is to be seen here; a much more advantageous one than that by the noble historian, who paints him "insolent, imperious, flattering, dissembling, had courage enough not to fail, where it was absolutely necessary, and had no impediment of honour to restrain him from doing anything that might gratify any of his passions".

This description of the Duke is probably just enough, since his treatment of Midside Maggie was one of the few generous gestures recorded in his favour and he was even famed as a false coiner, so that a local saying was: "Like a Lauderdale bawbee, as bad as can be." He was a strange mixture, mostly bad, and it was perhaps as well that he died childless, the title lapsing when he was succeeded by his brother, the 3rd Earl of Lauderdale, through whom the present 16th earl is descended.

Pennant's mention of the inside as "heavily stuccoed" is a remarkably weak description of the magnificent ornate ceilings which are amongst the finest of the Restoration period. As well as the Lely there is also a considerable collection of pictures, amongst which a particularly delightful Guardi caught my eye. Singularly incongruous, at first sight, are the fireplaces of Aberdeen granite in the hall and panelled room downstairs, which must surely be a nineteenth-century addition. Amongst the many museum pieces was the silver spade used by the Countess of Lauderdale in 1899 to inaugurate the founding of the Lauderdale Light Railway, which ceased to exist in the 1930s.

The difficulties of keeping up a house of this nature, which is already a museum, must be considerable. Some idea of its size can be gained when it is appreciated that during the first world war it was a hospital and during the second a girls' school, but on both occasions the family still remained in residence. Amongst the most pleasing features to me were the parks and policies enhanced by the mares and yearlings of Captain de Warrenne Rogers's well-known stud, which is based in the stables.

It sometimes seems as if almost every building, every town and village, as well as every hill and valley in the Borders has its tale of violent death, rape or slaughter. Lauder, a trig little town, notable according to a nineteenth-century gazetteer as having two streets "bearing the absurd names of the Upper and Under Backsides", is no exception. Pennant's account of the matter is brief but interesting enough:

Lauder, a small town, noted for an insolent act of justice done by the nobility on the upstart favourites of James III, Cochran, a mason, created Earl of Mar, Hommil, a taylor, Leonard, a smith, Rogers, a musician, and Torfisan, a fencing master, directing all his councils. The nobility assembled here with their vassals, in obedience to his majesties summons . . . took this opportunity to free themselves from these wretched ministers. They met in the church to consult the necessary measures; and while they were in debate, Cochran . . . knocked at the door to demand the cause of their assembly . . . he was seized . . . and with his comrades hanged over a bridge [now demolished] in sight of the king and the whole army.

In practice, one gathers, there had been some dissent amongst the nobles about what action to take. Lord Gray, perhaps to spur the rest on, recounted the fable of the mice who met to discuss ways and means of dealing with an obnoxious cat and agreed to tie a bell round its neck to give warning of its movements, but lacked the courage to do so. At that Archibald, Earl of Angus, a man of powerful build, sprang up enraged:

"I am he," he cried, "who will bell the cat."

At that particularly inauspicious moment, Cochrane came knocking at the door, and he and his companions were summarily siezed by the nobles, led by the Earl of Angus, and hung, as Pennant described. It is perhaps understandable that ever afterwards the Earl of Angus was known as 'Bell-the-cat' Archibald. If the experience of 'Tarbrush' is anything to go by it is probable that to his intimates he was latterly known simply as 'Bell'.

Such scenes of sudden death and rough justice were common throughout the confused history of the Borders. It was not until the eighteenth and nineteenth centuries that they began to be more settled. James VI's determination to put an end to Border reiving, or cattle rustling, and to turn the Borders into his 'Middle Kingdom', although not at once entirely successful, was the turning point. From then onwards, the ways of the Borders grew more peaceful. The Border peel towers with their immensely thick walls, so necessary as a means of survival, which are still to be seen on both sides of the Cheviots and throughout the Border country, were gradually converted into dwelling houses, or allowed to fall into ruin. New mansions began to be built.

We drove on towards Mellerstain, perhaps the finest example of this purely domestic building during the eighteenth century. On the way we passed through Earlston, now to all intents and purposes a busy little manufacturing town, with tweed mills, saw mills and similar industries common to the Borders. Its strongest association, although questionable in the light of modern research, is with Thomas the Rhymer, or 'True Thomas', possibly Sir Thomas Learmont of Ercildoune, who was reputed to have lived in the thirteenth century and to have been spirited away for seven years by the Queen of the Fairies, who granted him the gift of prophecy. It is notable that with a few exceptions most of his prophecies were phrased in such general terms that they might be considered the result of clear thinking rather than actual prophetic powers. Obviously the same gift did not descend to the son of Earlston responsible for the two-foot-high white painted lettering on the railway bridge, which reads:

"ENGLISH GO HOME"

My companion, the East Anglian farmer, snorted with laughter at the sight of it.

"If the reverse was applied," he pointed out, "East Anglia would become even more underpopulated than the planners say it is at the moment. Every other farmer there's a Scot."

We passed the farm strangely named 'Sorrowless Field', so called, it is said, because it was the only farm for many miles which did not lose any men at Flodden. After a few miles of side roads we were soon driving down the magnificent beech avenue which leads to Mellerstain.

This is one of the great Adam houses of Scotland and perhaps the finest example in the Borders. The name most clearly associated with it is undoubtedly that of the wife of the man who originally started building the house in 1725, Lady Grizell Baillie, none other than the same Grizell who fed her father in the vault beneath Polwarth Church. She later married George Baillie and her dominant chin can be seen in many portraits inside the house.

Through marriage to her daughter, the family of the Earl of Haddington inherited the estate and completed the building of the house in the grand Adam style. For all that, it is fascinating to walk round this house and observe from the family portraits how the powerful Grizell jaw has descended almost unchanged through the generations since then. It is interesting also to note that the Earl of Haddington at the start of the nineteenth century was noted as an exponent of the latest agricultural methods, for this estate is still run in a manner which could be a model for almost any other in the country. Well-kept cottages, trim hedges, careful forestry and good farming all point to efficiency and care for detail as epitomised also in Lady Grizell's *Household Book*, which is still preserved and remains a classic piece of social history.

From Mellerstain it is a short cross-country journey to the upstanding mass of Hume Castle, visible as a landmark for many miles around (see pl. 5). As one approaches this square, uncompromising castellated pile the most incurious must begin to have some doubts. Surely those walls were not built for defence? It seems scarcely possible that such vast battlements could have been built for more than show. Nor, as one draws closer, does there seem to be any obvious entrance.

We drew up beside a small boy sucking a large lollipop.

"How do we get into the castle?" asked my friend.

"Ye'll hae tae get the key frae the sweety shop doon the brae," was the reply between sucks.

My friend did not at once start the car so the boy tried again. "The key's in the post office-suck-suck-down the hill."

Such ambivalence of speech is common to the Borders but my friend was so delighted with the translation that he insisted on presenting the urchin with sixpence for another lollipop. We then drove on to the small post office and after signing our names in the book and paying sixpence apiece for the privilege duly picked up the key. There followed a short climb from the road before we fitted the key into the worn wooden door and the mystery of Hume Castle was clear to us at last.

It is obvious at once, as soon as one is inside, that it is nothing more than a folly on a large scale. It resembles a Hollywood film mock-up of a castle. The vast battlements are merely false walls built on the site of an earlier ruined castle. For further information I referred to a nineteenth-century gazetteer:

The Castle properly does not exist; but the late Earl of Marchmont raised the walls from the ruins into which they had fallen and, by battlementing them, produced something like a castle, or what at least may pass for such at a distance.

The gazetteer also gives an interesting account of how the real castle, built in 1300, came to be a ruin. Cromwell had sent a Colonel Fenwick to capture it in 1650:

On arriving in the vicinity Colonel Fenwick drew up his men and sent the governor the following summons: "His Excellency, the Lord General Cromwell, hath commanded me to reduce this castle you now possess under his obedience, which if you now deliver into my hands for his service you shall have terms for yourself and those with you; if you refuse, I doubt not but in a short time, by God's assistance to obtain what I now demand. I expect your reply by seven of the clock tomorrow morning and rest your servant, George Fenwick." The governor, whose name was Cockburn, being it seems a man of some fancy, returned this quibbling answer: "Right Honourable—I have received a trumpeter of yours as he tells me, without a pass, to surrender Hume Castle to the Lord General Cromwell; please you, I never saw your General. As for Hume Castle it stands upon a rock. Given at Hume Castle this day before seven o clock. So resteth without prejudice to my native country, your most humble servant, T. Cockburn."

It seems that Cockburn added a postscript:

> I, Willie Wastle,
> Stand firm in my Castle,
> And a' the dogs in your town,
> Will no pull Willie Wastle down.

But all this was of no avail against Colonel Fenwick's batteries when they came into action. In the *Statistical Account* of 1792 the Rev. Alexander Duncan of Gordon recorded in a footnote:

A great grandmother of one of the present tenants of one of these farms told his neighbour, who died not many years ago, that she stood in her doorway and saw the walls of Hume Castle beat down by Oliver Cromwell's cannon.

It is clear from all this that in 1790 the Earl of Marchmont must have decided to be in the fashion, for in those days the rage for building 'romantick' edifices was sweeping the country. His contribution, which we can still see today, was an outstanding effort, in more ways than one.

Today there is a useful direction-finder erected in one corner by the Berwickshire Naturalist Society in 1931. Had it been there in 1804 it is doubtful if the 'Great False Alarm' would ever have arisen, for, used as an observation point in the Napoleonic, as well as both world wars, it was from here that the 'Alarm' originated. Apparently the watcher in Hume Castle was alerted by the fires of charcoal burners far down in Northumberland. Mistaking them for a signal beacon warning of invasion from Bamburgh on the coast, he lost his head and sparked off the alarm, which for a night plunged the Borders into a display of their old martial ardour.

On a clear day, the view from Hume Castle is very fine and it is possible to see right across the Merse of Berwickshire to the coast as far as Holy Island and Bamburgh Castle or even further. The rich land of the Merse and the fertile fields round Kelso must always have been an inviting target for raiders from the south. Referring once again to the Rev. Alexander Duncan, we find:

A rage for raising tobacco prevailed in 1782, and many acres of the best land were occupied with it, which diminished the crops of corn. But a bill, passed in Parliament in 1783 cured the frenzy. That bill allowed only 4d. the pound for the tobacco, though it was no illicit trade, whereas to many, 1s. the pound would scarcely have paid the price of the land rent, the expence of labour: &c.

The Rev. W. B. Daniel in his four-volume work *The Rural Sports* published in 1813 refers to this in more detail in his account of the county of Roxburghshire. He wrote:

As a piece of Agricultural History it may be remarked that

this County was at one time likely to become celebrated for the cultivation of Tobacco. Mr. Thomas Man, who had resided in America introduced it. The Product was declared by experienced Judges, to be equal in Quality, to any Tobacco brought from America; the Profits were amazing, it was not uncommon to procure in a season from one Acre, a Crop, which when cured was worth Seventy Pounds sterling; an Act of Parliament put a stop to its Culture. In the Parish of Crailing at the time when this Act was passed a Field of Thirteen Acres was sold with the young Crop on the Ground for three hundred and twenty pounds, but the Act interfering, the Farmer was compelled to dispose of his Tobacco to the Government at fourpence per pound, at which Rate the Produce was only one hundred and four pounds sterling. Both Soil and Climate were extremely favourable for the Growth of Tobacco, which might have been brought to a high degree of perfection. The Plants grow best in a light Soil, well manured, they were reared in Hot-Beds and set at the Distance usually allowed to Cabbages, and for clearing the Land, Tobacco answered all the purposes of a Green Crop.

Approaching Kelso from the direction of Hume Castle, we called by appointment on Mr. T. Laing, who farms at Harrietfield Farm on the outskirts of the town. I had been informed that in his house he had a cockpit, which was well worth seeing as a feature of unusual architectural interest; but I had no clear idea of what to expect. With memories of Mark Twain and similar authors I vaguely visualised a room on the ground floor with a sunken pit in the centre of it.

From the outside the whitewashed farmhouse has little to distinguish it from many similar handsome and attractive houses built during the eighteenth century. Mr. Laing greeted us and led us, rather to my surprise, upstairs. In the centre of the house on the first floor was a corridor approached by a short flight of stairs. To my further surprise, he bent down and with the help of his son raised these stairs, which hinged upwards, exposing an opening about four foot six inches high, yawning blackly under the corridor. It was only then that it dawned on me that this was a secret cockpit.

Mr. Laing switched on a light inside the opening which revealed a tunnel extending under the corridor. Bent double, we went forward for about fifteen feet to find that it opened into a room at the end, brightly lit by a naked bulb. There was no sunk pit in this case, such as I had expected. This was just a room some fourteen foot across by twenty-four in length and four foot six high. Round the walls about a foot from the floor-boards was a wide bench fixed to the wall. Sitting on it, one's head nearly touched the beams supporting the floor of the room above.

It was easy to picture the sort of scenes that must have taken place there many times. Around the room, filling the benches, the cockfighting supporters of Kelso in the secret would be leaning forward, eagerly placing their bets and cheering on their champion. In the space in the centre the two owners would be anxiously watching as the candles flickered and the cocks fought their mains, bloody spurred and beady eyed, game to the last.

As cockfighting was finally declared illegal in 1849, this extraordinary concealed cockpit must have been clandestinely built some time after that date. Presumably it was done by local carpenters who were in the secret. One would imagine that it must have been difficult to keep it secret for very long, but it seems to have been done successfully, for not even the Laings, who have been there since the turn of the century, have any record of when it was built or when a main was last held. It now serves the prosaic function of spare boxroom, though, as Mrs. Laing pointed out, the inconvenience of opening the heavy trapdoor in the stairway each time it is required weighs against its usefulness in that respect. For all that, it must be almost unique in the Borders.

We drove on towards Kelso. Pennant wrote: "The environs of Kelso are very fine: the lands consist of gentle risings

4. "Polwarth church—bears a strange resemblance from a distance to a child's toy church built of bricks" (p. 21)

5. "Hume Castle, visible as a landmark for many miles around . . . this square, uncompromising castellated pile" (p. 32)

6. "John Rennie's bridge, built in 1803 as a model for Waterloo bridge." Kelso (p. 38)

7. "The castle on its Motte—first built by Bishop Flambard in 1121." Northam castle from a print c. 1830 (p. 54)

enclosed with hedges and extremely fertile." Of the town he noted: "Enter that neat place, built much after the manner of a *Flemish* town with a square and town house. It contains about twenty-seven hundred souls, has a very considerable market, and great quantities of corn are sold here weekly, by sample." He regretted "my not arriving in time to see the races".

As regards the population, the *Statistical Account* of 1792, written by Dr. Christopher Douglas, noted:

Population. The return from Dr. Webster in 1755 was 2781 and the number at present amounts to 4324 . . . In 38 years the increase of inhabitants has been 1534. This great increase may, in part, be accounted for, from the destruction of many villages in the neighbourhood, occupied by small farmers and mechanics. From the enlargement of the farms, many were obliged to follow other trades, and Kelso being the metropolis of the district, they flocked there for habitations and employment; and, in proportion as labourers and mechanics have become fewer in the country, Kelso increased in population.

The effects of the improvements in agriculture during the eighteenth century led to increasing enclosures and the amalgamation of many small farms in larger holdings. The labourers and small farmers thus forced off the land went to the nearest town. Today the improvements in mechanisation on the farms are resulting in less labour being required, and at the same time the present trend is once again towards larger farms and the smaller man is being forced off the land through sheer economic pressure. The only difference today is that instead of moving to the nearest towns the drift is towards the larger cities and centres of population.

Since its considerable expansion of population in the eighteenth century Kelso has remained fairly constant at about 4,000. Owing to its large square it gives the illusion of being a much larger town than it really is. Behind the square only the west end (see pl. 6) remains standing of what must have once been one of the finest Border abbeys before it was destroyed by the Earl of Hertford leading Henry VIII's forces against the Scots in 1545.

Kelso is closely associated with Sir Walter Scott, who went to the grammar school there for a brief period in 1783, where he met the ill-fated Ballantyne brothers who were later to be his publishers and partners in business. It is still an attractive town and many people have commented on the similarity between the large cobbled square and a French *place*. Never for a moment, however, could one mistake the Borderers thronging the pavements for their Gallic counterparts.

To my mind, the time to visit Kelso is not for the races, which are still held bi-annually, but for the spring or autumn horse sales held each year in Springwood Park on the other side of the Tweed from the town. Then the Borderers' natural love of a horse asserts itself. Horses and horse boxes converge on Kelso from all points of the compass. The jingle of bits and the clatter of hooves on cobblestones awake the echoes as they cross the square and stream over Rennie's bridge, built in 1803 as a model for the Waterloo Bridge, to replace an earlier bridge swept away by the Tweed in spate.

From as far south as Yorkshire, from Northumberland, Cumberland and from all over the Borders they come, drawn by a common interest. Sheep farmers, huntsmen, horse copers and county, their forefathers reived each other's cattle and fought each other bloodily. For all that they were generally ready with their wit, with an apt nickname, or a tossed-off piece of doggerel verse, and above all they were tough. Here is a cross-section of the Borders and, studying the weatherbeaten faces, good-humoured, scowling, shrewd, dour, open or oafish, one feels that time has not changed them greatly.

CHAPTER 3

Kelso to Holy Island

Said Tweed tae Till
What gars ye rin sae still?
Said Till tae Tweed,
Though ye rin wi' speed
And I rin slaw,
Where ye droun ae man
I droun twa.

TRADITIONAL SAW

CLOSE TO Kelso is Floors Castle. Colonel Thornton, visiting Kelso in 1784, referred to it as follows:

Fleurs, the seat of the Duke of Roxburgh, which is a pleasant walk from the town. The approach to the house is not finished; when complete it will be very handsome. The house itself is an old one modernised, and more has been made of it than of any I have seen altered . . . The view to the south, commanding part of the town of Kelso, with the abbey, the bridge and the country beyond, with the river Tweed and Tiviot uniting, forms a desirable landscape.

Built originally by Vanbrugh, the architect of Blenheim, in 1718 it is still the family seat of the Duke of Roxburghe. It was re-designed by Playfair in 1848 and so much has now 'been made of it' that it is reputed to be the largest lived-in house in the country. It has been battlemented with a determination and regularity which brings to mind a child's toy fort. The effect at close quarters is somewhat overpowering.

39

Contrary to what I had previously been told, the house is only opened to the public once a year for charity, but the grounds may be visited once a week. From the Factor's office overlooking Kelso Square we received a card on which was printed: "This card admits on Wednesdays only from 10 to 4 o'clock. Motors to enter at the Second Lodge, and park at Castle Stables." Although these may sound comparatively simple instructions we managed to lose our way in the extensive grounds where the well-grown trees and numbers of pheasants showing in the coverts indicated the likelihood of some good shooting during the season.

Eventually, driving past the house, we found the stables, battlemented in keeping with the rest. One part of the large cobbled yard had clearly been converted into modern garages. Instinctively I turned in the opposite direction in search of the head groom, an Irishman named Sullivan, whom Captain de Warrenne Rogers had recommended me to meet. A lightweight whipcord Dickensian character, like most keen horsemen he was pleased to have an opportunity to show off his charges to someone genuinely interested. Quite aside from the fact that these were splendid horses he is obviously an outstanding horse handler. I have never seen stallions more amenable and their appearance did him credit. The Duke may have given up hunting but he appears to be fortunate in his employees.

"The view to the south", as Thornton noted, is particularly fine. Almost all the stretches of the Tweed valley are pleasing to the eye, but this is perhaps amongst the most delightful. It is also, incidentally, probably amongst the most profitable from a leasing viewpoint. The pick of the fishing in the Tweed lies between Coldstream and Melrose and Kelso is almost midway between the two.

If the cost of salmon fishing on the Tweed is notoriously high there is good reason for it. When spinning for salmon, down river from Kelso, in 1936, Lady Joicey caught twenty-six salmon and two sea trout in a single marathon February day's fishing. Allowing for kelts, she caught and landed thirty-four fish. Since the average weight of these fish was over nine pounds and the time normally allowed for playing a fish is reckoned to be about a minute per pound it would seem that Lady Joicey was engaged in playing fish solidly for rather more than six hours. Presuming that it would be dark by four and that she started around ten her time was thus very fully occupied.

Even for the Tweed this is exceptional, but it is a river which is improving from year to year rather than deteriorating. Unlike many rivers the seasonal catches now are very much better than they were fifty years ago. Through uncontrolled netting and poaching, especially the vicious 'leistering', or spearing of spawning salmon by torchlight, condoned and even extolled by Scott and his friend Scrope, author of *Days and Nights of Salmon Fishing on the Tweed*, the river was in a parlous state as far back as 1850.

It was only the 1857 Tweed Act, followed by the Scottish Salmon Fisheries Act of 1868, which saved the day. The Tweed was the subject of Acts of Parliament as far back as 1768 and 1771 when the first Tweed Acts limited the net fishing boundary to five miles off the estuary. There were five more Tweed Acts of varying degrees of effectiveness before the 1857 Act. This Act resulted in the formation of the Tweed Commission, the first effective governing body. The Commissioners are the 250 riparian owners. They act through a Superintendent, whose duty it is to supervise the whole area.

I met Colonel R. M. Ryan, the Superintendent, by appointment, at his bachelor home on the Rutherford estate near Kelso. Middle-aged, powerfully built and of medium height, wearing a fisherman's blue jersey and open-necked shirt, he had the deeply tanned face of a man out in all weathers He ushered me into the comfortable chaos of papers and books in his study and I took a seat while his terrier bitch sniffed my trousers with interest.

"What sort of size of area do you cover?" I began.

41

"One thousand eight hundred and seventy square miles," he replied quite casually.

"That includes thirty miles up the coast and seven miles south as well as five miles out to sea," he amplified. "Apart from that all the tributaries which run into the Tweed are included."

"In fact your area includes England as well?"

"Oh, yes, of course. After all the first three miles of the Tweed are entirely in England and for the first fifteen miles one bank is English. Then there are the tributaries, such as the Till, which run entirely in England."

I was beginning to realise that looking after the ninety-seven miles of the Tweed involved a great deal more than I had imagined.

"What exactly is the scope of your duties?" I asked.

"Control of netting and rod fishing, control of poaching and pollution and all other aspects of pisciculture."

"Do you get much poaching?"

"Oh, yes. Quite enough."

"What staff do you have?"

"Ten full-time bailiffs and seventy to eighty special bailiffs."

We went on to discuss drift netting. Colonel Ryan had had to give evidence before the Hunter Committee as to the damage done to the salmon fishing by drift netting, that is by trawlers fishing at night some twenty miles off the mouth of the Tweed. He was careful to make it clear that he regarded a well-run netting industry as an asset to a river and he spoke highly of the Berwick Salmon Fisheries Company. I could not, however, entirely accept his subsequent statement that letting a stretch of fishing on the Tweed was not necessarily a paying proposition. He argued that the overheads of ghillies and boats almost counterbalanced the rent. On the other hand, as I pointed out, this depends on the rent.

The Tweed fishing boats, incidentally, are blunt-ended with a revolving stool seat for the fisherman in the stern. They are modelled on the cobles used at the mouth of the Tweed and down the coast of Northumberland for seine netting. No outboard motors are allowed. No boats therefore are used on much more than quarter-mile stretches. This does admittedly add to the costs involved, but against that the rents are high, amounting sometimes to as much as four hundred pounds or more for a rod per week.

Colonel Ryan's strong jaw and incisive answers to my questions made me feel that he was a man I would rather have on my side in any fight, either verbal or physical. It was possible to feel almost sorry for any poacher who crossed his path. It is not surprising that the Tweed is widely regarded as one of the best run rivers in Europe.

By the roadside between Rutherford and Kelso is a massive grass-covered mound, which is all that remains of Roxburgh Castle, strategically placed between the Tweed and the Teviot. Captured and held by the English for nearly a hundred years of almost continual warfare, it was besieged in 1460 by James II of Scotland. While watching his cannons in action "mair cureious nor becam him or the majestie of ane king . . . his thie bone was doung in twa with ane piece of ane misframit gun that brak in the schutting". With his femoral artery severed he cannot have lived more than thirty seconds. His widow, however, had his son crowned James III in Kelso Abbey and continued the siege, finally demolishing the castle when it was taken. In the grounds of Floors there is reputed to be a holly tree marking the scene of James II's death.

In spite of the size of Floors, which is very obvious from across the river, the Duke of Roxburghe's estate is by no means the largest in the Borders. Yet although it is only in the region of fifty thousand acres with a good deal lying towards the Cheviots and the Border, there is little that is marginal land. The Duke has also now extended his estates into the Highlands and, even more unusually, over the Cheviots into Northumberland, outbidding the Duke of Northumberland

43

for an estate recently on the market. Border reiving and rivalry with the Percies, it would seem, have not altogether ceased, even if it now takes more modern forms.

I mentioned Colonel Ryan's suggestion that fishing rents might only just cover costs, to the Duke's factor, Mr. Bachelor, and his eyebrows nearly disappeared. Dressed in a tweed knickerbocker shooting suit his appearance was faintly Edwardian, but his reactions and outlook were modern enough. On this point he confirmed my views.

"That must, of course, depend on the rent, but you might say that here we have the cream of the cream of salmon fishing."

In the circumstances I felt it would be tactless to enquire the cost of a beat on the Floors stretch of fishing, but the Junction Pool, especially, so named because it is formed by the junction of the Teviot with the Tweed, is notable for its record catches. It is only unfortunate today that with the commercialism which has now crept into salmon fishing much of the sporting element has, perforce, disappeared. If a man is paying a very large sum for his fishing he can no longer afford to treat the fish with the same altruistic sportsmanship. It has ceased to be a sport and become a business. In the process the pleasure has vanished unnoticed.

We drove out of Kelso towards Cessford Castle, the ancient seat of the Kers of Cessford, from whom the Duke of Roxburghe is descended. On the way the name Sunlaws caught my eye on the map and an entry in the *Statistical Account* which had interested me sprang to mind. The Rev. Andrew Bell, Minister of Roxburgh in 1792, wrote about some caves:

cut out of solid rock, in the middle of a high precipice, whose bottom is washed by the Teviot, which flows here broad and deep in a serpentine form. Three of these caves have been of large dimensions. One of them was used as a hiding place for horses in 1745 . . . and is called the Horse Cave. Another, whose mouth is almost quite filled up, and inaccessible now,

44

reaches so far back into the ground, that old people who have been in it say they have never got to the farthest end of it, and suppose this cave had been a subterraneous passage to Sunlaws mansion house in times of danger. A third is called the Dove Cave, from its having been used by Lady Chatto as a pigeon house.

Unfortunately we did not have time to investigate these caves and there remains the opportunity for some keen potholer to check the accuracy of this account. There is no reason to doubt that there is a concealed cave of some size, but the Rev. Bell was inclined to make the most of matters as another extract shows:

Memorials of death and slaughter appear in many parts of this parish, from human bones, sometimes scattered in the open field uncoffined; sometimes huddled together head to foot, in a hole in the earth, and covered with rugged stones; and sometimes found in cells of mouldering towers, with instruments of murder in their bowels.

We drove on through Eckford. The church there has a Dead Watch Tower prominent in its graveyard, mute reminder of the days of the body snatchers, when it was necessary to keep watch over fresh graves to prevent the bodies being stolen for medical research. By way of side roads we finally reached the solid red stone remains of Cessford Castle. In 1792 in the *Statistical Account* the Rev. William Paton wrote restrainedly: "From those parts of the walls yet entire it appears to have been a place of considerable strength." He added a footnote:

According to tradition there was a subterranean vault for concealing persons and goods within its walls, to which access was got by only one aperture, which was opened or shut, as seemed necessary, by a large stone with an iron ring in it. This stone and the ring have been seen by some persons still alive, but the entrance to the peel or dungeon is now chocked with rubbish.

45

It has been supposed that this 'subterranean vault' may have been connected by an underground passage with a cave in the bank of Cessford burn to the north, which was known as Habbie Ker's cave. Use of such a passage might explain how the Earl of Surrey, leading Henry VIII's forces in 1545, successfully took this apparently impregnable fortress. It would also explain his otherwise enigmatic remark, "It might never have been taken had the assailed been able to go on defending."

The interior is still considerably 'chocked up' with accumulated mounds of debris. The twelve-foot-thick walls, though now split, are still impressive. With something of a struggle it is possible to climb to the first floor and the views towards Morebattle, Yetholm and the Cheviot foothills are splendid. It is easy to see what a strategic position this was, straddling the route taken by the English invaders on their way to plunder the rich lands around Kelso. It is a pity that more effort is not made to preserve this massive ruin, which is still owned by the Duke of Roxburghe, the descendant of the Kers.

Notorious as freebooters, reivers and fighters, as well as for their blood feud with the Scotts of Buccleuch, the Kers of Cessford, like the Kers of Ferniehurst, were famed in Border history and battles. In 1606, poacher-turned-gamekeeper Sir Robert Ker, then Warden of the Scottish Middle Marches, was made Lord Roxburghe and later the ducal title came into being. After passing twice through the female line the family name is now Innes Ker.

We drove on through Morebattle, a rather attractive stone-built village with some interesting looking old houses. In 1792 the valley beyond contained "a loch of more than a mile in circumference, in which are both pike and perch". This was finally drained in the early nineteenth century and now one drives along a lush valley to the Yetholms, Town Yetholm and Kirk Yetholm, lying each side of the Bowmont at the foot of the Cheviots.

Perhaps I made the mistake of expecting too much of the

46

Yetholms. So much ballyhoo has been written about them as the great centre of the Faa tribe of gypsies that unconsciously I may have been expecting gaily coloured horse-drawn caravans with flashing-eyed dark-skinned beauties ready to tell one's fortune when their palm was crossed with silver. This was the 'romantic' picture conjured up by the rose-coloured magic of Sir Walter Scott and his Victorian successors.

It is a sound corrective to read the Rev. William Blackie's description in the *Statistical Account*:

The parish has, I suppose, more than doubled its population in the course of this century, because many villages in the neighbouring parishes of Hounam, Morbottle and Linton, have been totally razed since the memory of people now living, and many of the inhabitants have withdrawn into the towns of Yetholm and Kirkyetholm.

He noted especially: "Occupations of the inhabitants: Tinkers and gypsies, and in Kirk-Yetholm, including women and children, 50."

This scarcely sounds as if there was any large body of gypsies resident in Kirk Yetholm and in practice they appear merely to have owned a few cottages granted to them as winter quarters by Captain Bennet of Marlefield in return for recovering a valuable stolen horse. For all that the Yetholm tribe of Faa seems to have been dominant throughout Northumberland, Berwickshire and Roxburgh, so that Yetholm was an ideal centre. Towards the west, around Langholm, was the rival tribe of Baillie.

In 1847 several hundred gypsies were said to have assembled at the 'crowning' of Esther Faa, the last 'Queen' of the gypsies. Before she died, in 1883, she declared: "There are nane o' my seed, breed, or generation in Yetholm." Such was the Victorian urge for the 'picturesque', however, that besides several hundred gypsies at her funeral the roads were blocked by several thousand spectators.

Today many gypsies have given up the unequal struggle

against conformity and have accepted life in new housing estates. Those who remain on the roads are harried from pillar to post and county to county by the police. Most of them have taken to motor-driven vans, rather than the old horse-drawn caravans. Those few who defiantly continue in their old ways are still, as they ever were, dirty, thievish and clannish, without a shred of real romance to them, but their occasional appearances around the countryside are at least an assurance that individualism can still survive in spite of an increasingly rigid planned pattern of state living.

There was no sign of gypsies in either of the Yetholms when we visited them. Town Yetholm is the larger of the two, with a spacious main street. There are one or two cottages remaining and one, with a brand-new thatch and wrought-iron sign displaying the words 'Rose Café', might have been planted in any Surrey village without comment. We wondered whether Town Yetholm is becoming a self-conscious tourist trap, or whether, like Kirk Yetholm with its pleasant green, some of the cottages have been taken over and 'renovated' by elderly retired people in search of somewhere to end their days in peace. In either event there is always a danger of too much paint, as on the face of a woman, obscuring a natural beauty.

On the night of the famous "False Alarm", the Yetholms mustered 188 volunteers. The schoolmaster, one of the officers, noticed a woman in the ranks:

"What are you doing here, Bella?" he demanded. "This is no place for a woman."

"I'll aye tak' a bullet afore ma bairns," retorted Bella. "Here I am an' here I stay."

We drove on above the Bowmont, skirting the foothills of the Cheviots and soon crossing the Border (marked by a red cross), and then entered the Northumberland National Park marked with the sign of a curlew in black on a white background. Not a great deal further on we passed a large sign: 'Ware Hounds', followed by an equally large 'Thank You'.

Such signal politeness deserved attention, but the College Valley Hounds merit attention for their sterling qualities as well. Their blood is to be found in many other famous packs, especially in the Borders.

Here one is in the heart of the Border hunting country. North-west are the Lauderdale, north-east the Berwickshire, west the Duke of Buccleuch's, south-west the Jedforest, east the North Northumberland, the Percy and Colonel Milvaine's over by the coast. Concentrated in such a comparatively small area this makes an impressive number. No doubt this is one way that the old reiving instincts can be safely consummated today.

We drove on and turned up the College valley itself. The estate of Hethpool here, which is thought to have the oldest peel tower in the Borders in its grounds, was once owned by Admiral Lord Collingwood, who served with Nelson at Trafalgar. He wrote in 1828: "What I am most anxious about is the plantation of oaks in the country. We shall never cease to be a great people while we have ships, which we cannot have without timber . . . I plant an oak wherever I have a place to put it in." The large grove of trees visible at the foot of the hill above Hethpool are known as 'the Collingwood Oaks', but as he had the single-minded and rather engaging habit of wandering round with a bag of acorns in his pocket, which he planted wherever he saw a likely spot, almost any of the mature oaks in the district may owe their origin to him.

We were told that if we followed up the College burn, we might chance on a herd of wild goats which live up on the slopes of the Cheviots. Apparently there is a herd of over a score of them which can often be seen thereabouts. From a photograph we were shown of these beasts they certainly have impressive sweeping ibex-like horns. Rather reluctantly we decided not to go goat-hunting that day, but somehow a herd of wild goats seemed entirely justifiable and perfectly fitting in those surroundings.

49

This is an area where a strong pre-Norman Saxon influence still exists. In the pleasant withdrawn village of Kirknewton there is a Norman church possibly built on the site of an earlier Saxon one erected by Paulinus, the Christian missionary of the seventh century. On the wall a carving, probably of Saxon origin, shows the Virgin surrounded by kilted Magi, in those days most likely the garb of every Northumbrian. By the side of the road a carved stone tablet mounted on a concrete base commemorates the baptism of several thousand Northumbrians by Paulinus in the nearby river Glen.

It was near here that King Arthur was reputed to have fought the first of his twelve major battles. The Borders area is steeped in Arthurian legend and during the subsequent twelve centuries it was steeped in blood. Notably bloody, and even after four and a half centuries still the battle most grievously remembered by the Scots, was Flodden, also fought nearby.

On the subject of Flodden it is particularly interesting to note that there is no contemporary Scottish version of the battle. There are no less than three contemporary accounts of the English side, but it is reasonable to assume a certain bias about them. No Scottish account was written by a competent eye-witness at the time, for the very good reason that they were almost without exception killed. The King, James IV, his son, ten earls, thirteen barons, ninety chiefs of families and four hundred members of the nobility were killed on the Scottish side. The number of Scots dead was estimated at over 6,000, while the English losses were only 1,500. Why and how did it happen?

In 1513 Henry VIII had invaded France and Louis XII had appealed to James to attack the English rear as a distraction. Partly no doubt to assist the 'auld ally' and partly also perhaps with a view to plunder and to pay off old scores James assembled 30,000 men outside Edinburgh and marched over the Border on August 22nd. He captured the castles of Norham, Wark, Etal, Ford and Chillingham without difficulty, and by the end of August had entrenched himself on Flodden Edge, the hill above Ford. There he settled down to await the English forces, who do not seem to have reached Wooler until the 8th of September under their seventy-year-old leader, Thomas Howard, Earl of Surrey (subsequently created Duke of Norfolk as a reward for his victory), and his son the Lord High Admiral, Thomas Howard.

The crux of the battle, which took place late in the afternoon of the 9th of September, appears to have been James's failure to prevent the English flanking force under Lord Thomas Howard from crossing the Twizel bridge over the Till. He then appears to have come down from the heights and engaged the English in a position much more favourable to them than to him. On the face of it Flodden seems to have been a colossal blunder, but there is one perfectly sound explanation for James's failure to realise in time that the English were encircling him. Twizel bridge, a narrow handsome single arch, which still spans the Till today as it did then, is out of sight from the heights in a fold of the ground. Furthermore the weather had been extremely bad and during the day a drizzle was falling. Anyone who knows these east coast haars, or mists, will appreciate that this could very easily explain why James lost touch with his foes.

When he realised, too late, what was happening, he then obviously decided, again too late, to attack Lord Thomas Howard's forces before the Earl of Surrey could join him. At first the Socttish left wing under Lord Home completely defeated the Admiral's right, but the Scots then set about plundering and took no further part in the battle. The Admiral, supported at this critical juncture by Lord Dacre's Borderers from Cumberland, charging behind the 'Red Bull' of Dacre defeated the Scots in front of him and then swung round to assist the Earl of Surrey by attacking the remainder in flank and rear. Caught thus in a pincer movement, it was in the ensuing desperate mêlée that the Scots suffered their grievous losses.

Today a simple granite cross stands by the roadside on the hill above the village of Branxton, the supposed site of the battle. On it are carved the words: 'Flodden. To the Brave of Both Nations' and the date 1513. I say supposed site advisedly because it seems to me that such a battle was likely to have straggled quite considerably. Looking at the ground today, wooded, well drained and well tilled, it is hard to imagine it as it must have been then, a treeless waste of heather and boggy marshland.

We turned from the scene of Flodden towards Wark Castle on the banks of the Tweed. This was the sentinel of the East March of England facing Hume Castle on the Scottish side. From the twelfth to the sixteenth century it had a history of "surprises, assaults, sieges, blockades, surrenders, evacuations, burnings, restorations and slaughters" almost without parallel even in the hectic history of the Borders. After raiding Roxburgh in 1460 the Scots dealt in much the same way with Wark, although it was repaired by the English only to be demolished again before Flodden and subsequently partly repaired once more. Finally with the Union, it was allowed to decay and today, as with Roxburgh, little more remains than a large grass-covered mound on which the children from the nearby village school were playing.

It was here that the historian Froissart placed the legendary court scene when the Countess of Salisbury's garter unfortunately came undone and lay in full view of the court. King Edward III bent down to pick it up and to rebuke those of the court who tittered at his action uttered the enigmatic reproof, "*Honi soit qui mal y pense.*" (Evil be to him who evil thinks.) He then tied the garter round his own knee and thus supposedly instituted the Honourable Order of the Garter.

It is strange to realise that here the Tweed forms the actual Border line. On the other hand, this does constitute a barrier of some sort, whereas the gap between the Tweed and the Cheviot foothills has no natural barriers. It is easy thus to appreciate the strategic significance of Wark Castle in the eyes of both sides. It is also easy to understand that no one who lived in these parts was likely to take the Border line very seriously. It would always have been a simple matter to slip over in a small raiding party and return with cattle or sheep under cover of the hours of darkness. Small wonder that for centuries, on both sides of the Border, wise men lived in walled keeps and locked up their cattle by night.

On the north side of the river beyond Wark is Sir Alec Douglas-Home's estate, the Hirsel. On the north side, also, is Coldstream, home of the Guards regiment of that name, raised originally by General Monk in 1660. Apart from this the town was once famous, like Lamberton Toll and Gretna Green, for its runaway marriages, performed by the toll-keeper on the bridge. Evident now is a quiet pride that the first Border Prime Minister should be so intimately connected with the town.

We crossed the Till by way of the same Twizel bridge used by Admiral Lord Howard before Flodden. In 1962, not far from here, a gang of poachers were caught redhanded by the Tweed bailiffs with twenty-nine fish after using cyanide to poison the water. When brought before the court in Wooler in due course they escaped with fines amounting to less than £100.

As I wrote once before* unfortunately the 1951 Salmon and Freshwater Protection Act, although allowing for confiscation of the car and apparatus, as well as the imprisonment of proven poachers, left plenty of legal loopholes and proved no deterrent to those who receive poached fish. It should be understood that there is nothing in the very least glamorous about this sort of poaching. It is organised vandalism as well as theft, for once a river has been poisoned all the young fish and plant life are destroyed and it may take up to ten years to recover. The poachers themselves are the sort of riff-raff who would probably turn their hand to other petty crimes if poaching were not so easy and so profitable. The regrettable feature hitherto has been

*Soho for the Colonel (MacGibbon & Kee, 21s.).

E

the reluctance of many sheriffs to punish the offenders heavily enough when they have been caught. Only when the courts deal strongly with them will this sort of thing stop.

We turned off to inspect the village of Norham, which lies in a bend of the Tweed, at the site of one of the first fords above Berwick. It is a most attractive old village with a green and a cluster of stone-built slate-roofed houses grouped around it and the ancient church (see pl. 7). Beyond lies a broad street of feudal proportions leading up the hill to the castle on its Motte. The old stone houses, ivy- and lichen-covered, give the unmistakeable impression of having first taken root with the coming of the Normans, gnarled and mellow now maybe, but unchanged and unchanging.

The entire setting delights the eye as much with its charm as with its total unexpectedness. On the other side of the Tweed is Scotland. Here, right on the Border, is something as unmistakeably English as a Beefeater in the Tower of London. Here, one feels, lies a Norman gentleman recumbent, slumbering, but watchful still.

Norham was once, strangely enough, part of the powerful County Palatine of Durham, within which the Bishops of Durham, as Lords Palatine, exercised the rights normally enjoyed by the king. The castle was first built by Bishop Flambard in 1121. Although it changed hands a number of times, such was its natural strength that it was seldom captured. Prior to Flodden, it was reduced by the use of cannon, including Mons Meg, now in Edinburgh Castle. Subsequently repaired, it was slowly allowed to fall into ruin before finally being placed in the hands of the Ministry of Works in 1923. It is worth exploring for its massive inner ward and keep, but it struck me as one of the most dangerous ruins I have visited and definitely not to be recommended for children. The provision of a few more guard rails would certainly not come amiss.

From Norham we made a cross-country journey to Haggerston Castle, from where it will be remembered that Sir William

Haggerston rode with his volunteers to Berwick on the fateful night of the "False Alarm". The Haggerston family, one of the oldest in Northumberland, is now no more and the castle appears to have suffered a number of startling changes in the past few decades.

The old castle was supplanted, as was often the way in the late nineteenth century, by a much more elaborate building, including a massive 110-foot water tower, a rotunda, and an ornamental lake. After the 1914–18 war it seems there was a hiatus when the building was partially demolished, except for the tower and the rotunda, and the estate sold. It was occupied by the army during the second world war and subsequently changed hands yet again. It was bought finally a decade ago by a Mr. Balfour and his go-ahead son, who decided to turn it into the caravan site it now is.

The point that struck me as soon as I visited the site was that here were caravans of a size I had never seen before. Vast glass-plated affairs nearly forty feet in length reposed like landborne houseboats on balloon tyres little larger than grossly inflated pram wheels. Clearly they could not be expected to travel far. It was only on querying this point that I realised for the first time that caravans over twenty feet long are illegal on the roads and can therefore only be moved on special transporters. They must in fact be found semi-permanent berths on sites throughout the country. Their advantage, apart from non-payment of rates, is that they can, at a pinch, be moved. It must also be admitted that some of these very large caravans appear to have every comfort imaginable.

We investigated the site. The water tower, dilapidated and mouldering, still dominates the entire area with some of the war-time barbed wire still keeping the curious at bay. A bar has been installed in the rotunda. Nearby is a shop providing all that campers are likely to require, from baked beans to toilet paper and soap. Further on is a new building reminiscent of an aircraft hangar with a large dance floor and air-conditioning humming softly like the inside of an aircraft-carrier. At the end is another bar where campers in shirt sleeves were having their morning glass of beer.

Mr. Balfour, silver-haired, high-coloured and portly, emerged from his small modern detached house in the grounds smoking a cigar and ready for his morning stroll round his grounds. We identified him—by his proprietorial air—without difficulty.

"Mr. Balfour, I presume?"

"Yes?"

We explained our interest in his site.

"How many acres have you here?"

"A hundred acres, plus swimming pool and ten acres of ponds and lakes," he replied expansively.

It is in every way, I suppose, a model for such sites. It was perhaps a mistake to arrive early in the morning, while the necessary jetsam of caravan life was being disposed of in the lines of the travelling caravans, as opposed to the more luxuriously ensconced semi-permanent lines. The effect was at first rather reminiscent of an overcrowded prefabricated housing site, but in the bar and by the lake it was abundantly clear that the caravanners were enjoying themselves. Mr. Balfour and his son are obviously supplying what the public wants.

We continued on to Holy Island.

CHAPTER 4

Holy Island to Alwinton

From the bonny bells of heather
They brewed a drink long-syne,
Was sweeter far than honey,
Was stronger far than wine.

R. L. STEVENSON, 1886

STRICTLY SPEAKING, Holy Island only just qualifies as an island since it can be approached dryshod at low tide. In shape it faintly resembles a badly drawn hand with a bulbous tip to the mile-long 'finger' pointing up the coast. This promontory, known as the Snook, stretches almost from east to west towards the mainland, which it approaches within a few hundred yards at the nearest point. The village at the opposite end of the island consists of two or three rows and squares of typical old Northumbrian houses, with a noticeable preponderance of inns. Apart from the harbour, the castle, the priory ruins and the church, that is about all; but there is a quiet charm, almost an enchantment about the place, which is unique.

The first record of Lindisfarne, as the Celts called it was in A.D. 634 when Oswald, the Christian King of Northumberland, gave it to Aidan, the Scots missionary bishop from Iona. Yet the name most closely associated with the island is that of another Scot, St. Cuthbert, who was a misogynist. According to Pennant the legendary reason for this was:

a charge of seduction brought against him by a certain princess, who was instantly punished by being swallowed up by the earth, which, on the intercession of the pacified saint, restored her to the king her father. From that time, not a woman was permitted to enter any church dedicated to the holy man.

In that respect St. Cuthbert appears to have been the forerunner of that type of Scots zealot, later familiar on the Border scene, who always persisted in carrying matters to excess. To escape women he retired to the almost inaccessible Farne Island further off the coast and went as far as refusing to allow any cows there. Subsequently, as Pennant noted, women were not even allowed in his shrine in Durham Cathedral, where his body finally came to rest.

Although Lindisfarne was sacked by the Danes soon after his death and was eventually evacuated for fear of further attacks, the priory (pl. 8) must have been restored by 1069 when the Bishop of Durham and his followers, of both sexes, took refuge there from the wholesale slaughter decreed in the north by William I. It was owing to its strong ties with the bishopric of Durham that Holy Island and the strip of coastline between there and Berwick, like Norham, became an isolated part of the palatinate, known as Islandshire.

Compared with these lively beginnings, the island's subsequent history was uneventful. It escaped being seriously raided by the Scots and in 1537 the priory was peacefully dissolved. The castle was built soon afterwards in Henry VIII's reign on a natural outcrop of basalt known as the Beblowe at the south-east of the island. Overlooking the approach to the harbour and about half a mile beyond the village, it was intended for coastal defence but never required. The population of around 200 have almost always lived by fishing and farming, though during the seventeenth and eighteenth centuries they provided their own quiet amusements in the shape of a little organised wrecking and smuggling. Since it was discovered as a 'watering place' in the mid-nineteenth century they have indulged in the normal tourist milking of any coastal resort.

It is only at high tide that the island is completely cut off from the mainland for a few hours. Yet, until a metalled causeway was built across to the nearest part of the Snook in 1958, access was difficult, being generally by decrepit old taxis, which were unharmed by the salt water, or on foot with an eye to tide and quicksand. The best approach has always been by boat, which preserves the illusion that it is truly an island.

From the hill above Fenwick, the line of low sand dunes spread out below against the dull blue-grey background of the sea with the castle rising theatrically at the far end resembles an artist's stage back cloth impression of an island far more than reality (see pl. 10). At close quarters this dream-like impression of having strayed into the middle of a Gilbert and Sullivan opera may still persist. It is all a little unreal. As well as being a place of enchantment with a charm all its own, Holy Island at times has a distinct flavour of comic opera about it.

We drove down to the causeway and consulted the tide tables there. Fortunately for us the tides were right for a three-hour visit. We drove across and along the firm sand beside the bent grass and dunes of the Snook, once a rabbit warren farmed for the bishopric, towards the small cluster of buildings visible in the distance.

We did not pause in the village, as our first objective was the castle. Bought in 1903 by the owner of *Country Life*, Mr. E. Hudson, it was restored by Sir Edwin Lutyens and in 1944 was given to the National Trust by Sir Edward de Stein. Although officially only open on Thursdays, we were fortunate that it was open on the Wednesday as well when we arrived.

Seen at close quarters perched on its tiny knoll of rock it is every bit as attractive as it appears at a distance. It is an almost absurdly pocket-sized castle. In estate agents' terms it might be described as a highly desirable *bijou* detached castlette. Manned by a total garrison of twenty at the most, it was briefly occupied by Royalist forces in 1643, but its capture by two Jacobites in 1715 was a classic story in keeping with the entire atmosphere of the island.

A certain Lance Errington, captain of a ship in the harbour, first reconnoitred the ground by demanding a shave from the guardian who doubled as local barber. Returning later with his nephew, Mark, on the pretext of having dropped his watch key, they suddenly produced loaded pistols and took over the castle, hoisting the Jacobite flag. Faced with lack of support and overwhelming odds they tried to escape, but were captured. Taken to Berwick gaol they escaped and slipped away to the Continent, eventually taking advantage of a general amnesty to return. Thus, in true comic opera tradition, all ended happily.

We went on from there to the priory ruins and thence to the church, where a friend with us, named Selby, was obviously interested to find memorials to his ancestors, once owners of the island and prominent in Northumbrian history for centuries. We then made a quick tour of the village itself, inspecting particularly a cross erected by a past Selby. We ended, or intended to, by renewing my acquaintance with Mr. Robert Kyle, the landlord of the Castle Inn, where the beer is still drawn straight from the wood.

Cox'n of the Holy Island lifeboat when I first knew him, he has now retired, sharing with his brother a notable record of forty-eight years such service. Although always assured that I was not born to be drowned, there was one occasion when I was remarkably pleased to see a lifeboat. I was a guest aboard a yacht which ended by drifting powerless and minus sails towards Norway before a full gale. Hence I have a lot of time for anyone connected with this voluntary and dangerous service. Mr. Kyle, however, had endeared himself to me by the answer he gave when asked in my hearing:

"How do you manage to live here in the winter?"

He looked his questioner solemnly in the eye.

"We live on the money you silly b . . . s spend in the summer," he replied.

Having exchanged this and other memories, I was surprised when he suggested that we should have a glass of mead.

"Mead?" I queried.

8. "The priory ruins." Holy Island (known to the Celts as Lindisfarne) from a print *c.* 1830 (p. 58)

9. "Kennelled in the old church." Colonel Milvaine's hounds at Belford (p. 62

10. "With the castle rising theatrically at the far end . . . resembles an artist's b
enchantment with a charm all its own, Holy Islan
11. "Beadnell is the only east coast harbour which actually faces

h impression of an island far more than reality. As well as being a place of
es has a distinct flavour of comic opera" (p. 59)
t—moored there are the old type of high prowed coble" (p. 67)

12. "On the bank a statue of Paulinus." The Lady's Well at Holystone (p. 80)

13. "The cream of the cream of salmon fishing." The Junction pool on the Tweed (p. 44)

"Oh, yes. We've started making that on the island since you were here last, you know," he replied. "Try some."

It seemed entirely in keeping with the atmosphere of Holy Island that if any industry had to be introduced it should be the unheard of but eminently suitable one of mead distilling. We agreed that it tasted like a Madeira flavoured with honey. The mead liqueur with a whisky base, which is also produced, probably tastes better than most sweet whisky liqueurs.

We were duly introduced to bearded Mr. Michael Hackett, the managing director and inventive genius behind this venture. Official taster to the Ancient Order of Mead Distillers, Mr. Hackett is an enthusiast and it is always pleasant to meet enthusiasts. Though not a native of the island, he comes from Durham, which is the next best thing. He led us into his small distillery—not much larger than a fair-sized two-car garage. There he expatiated on the processes involved as he matched colouring and blend in retorts and flasks. White-coated, surrounded by apparatus, his eyes glinting with enthusiasm behind his horn-rimmed spectacles and his teeth gleaming through his beard as he emphasised his points, Mr. Hackett was impressively like a film version of a mad scientist. There is nothing mad about his methods, however, for it is eloquent of their success that a much larger distillery is being built to keep pace with increasing demands.

There is much more, one gathers, to making mead than might at first be imagined. This is no haphazard business of gathering dew-soaked heather at dawn. Plastic tanks, refiners, strainers, corkers, bottlers and other impressive pieces of equipment surrounded us. The occasional 'glop, glop' of the mead fermenting in the vats standing in serried ranks resounded unexpectedly like the spasmodic chorus of bull frogs in a marsh. Perhaps fortunately, the smallest bonded warehouse in the country, which is attached to the distillery and holds the special Glenlivet whisky used in making the mead liqueur, was locked and sealed.

61

Even so, we only just left the island in time to cross the causeway before the tide caught us. We vowed to return in the winter months for wildfowling, either for widgeon on the splendidly named Cock of the Snook, or with a local guide for geese elsewhere, for the rip tide and quicksands have been the death of the unwary often enough in the past. In spite of its new industry and the influx of tourists that the causeway has brought, Holy Island remains largely unspoiled, especially in the winter months. Like most small islands, it has a closely integrated community much inter-related. They have no need for a policeman for instance because there is no law-breaking. Any 'cosh boy' who tried strong-arm tactics there would soon have short shrift. As is the case with most Northumbrian coastal fishermen, these people are tough and ready to stand up for themselves as they have for generations.

We drove on southwards through Belford. On the outskirts of this attractive small town we saw a pack of hounds turning into the entrance drive of a small square church by the roadside. On further investigation we found that the hounds, Colonel Milvaine's private pack until his death in the last decade and amongst the last private packs in the country, are actually kennelled in the old church. It has now been gutted and in the erstwhile vestry the bubbling corpses of braxy ewes stank strongly as the hounds' meat was prepared. They are a strong pack with a strain of College Valley and also of Cumberland hill hound (see pl. 9). The music they make in the church is certainly impressive.

Next door to the church is the home of a small farmer, Mr. Brown, who is opposed to hunting and will not allow hounds on his ground. Unlike the majority of merely noisy objectors he has produced his own alternative answer to foxes. He has invented a fox trap. This works on the principle that a dead chicken bait is hung above a pit filled with water. The fox reaches for it. This rings a warning bell in the house. A switch is then turned, which passes an electric current through the chicken, electrocutes the fox and causes it to fall into the pit. The theory is that if it is only stunned by the shock it will be drowned in the pit. Strange to relate it has been successful. Its application, however, is obviously too limited to be put forward as a serious alternative to hounds as a means of killing foxes.

From Belford we took the coast road which leads through attractive countryside to Bamburgh. Seen from a distance, Bamburgh Castle dominates the horizon and its massive bulk, covering a full quarter of a mile of upthrust basaltic rock, demands attention. If Holy Island was small here, one feels, is the grand-daddy of all castles, a noble Norman residence for chivalric knights, complete with all the usual offices, such as stabling and armouries and possibly with such desirable conveniences as jousting greens, all strategically placed on a rock 150 feet high. It towers above the straggling single village street and fills the skyline with its towers and battlements. It looks magnificent and is in fact little more than a folly.

The site itself is amongst the most ancient in Northumbrian history and, indeed, this is supposedly the castle that King Arthur gave to Sir Galahad. After many sieges and stirring events it had the doubtful distinction of being the first castle reduced to ruins by gunfire under attack by Edward IV in 1464 during the Wars of the Roses. Thereafter it was neglected by the Forsters, who owned it, and steadily allowed to decay until bought by Lord Crewe, Bishop of Durham and husband of Dorothy Forster, in 1704 as a stratagem to restore the ruined Forster family finances. He bequeathed it in trust for charitable purposes, but by 1894 the money in the trust was insufficient for upkeep and the trustees decided to sell. It was at this point that the Victorian armaments millionaire, Lord Armstrong of Cragside, founder of Vickers Armstrong, opened his *Times* at the breakfast table and read the news. Quite what insidious reasoning prompted him it is hard to say, but without more ado he announced to his startled family:

"I'm going to buy Bamburgh Castle."

He then went ahead and reputedly spent a million pounds on restorations, which involved almost rebuilding the castle as it was fancied that it had been. By 1900 when he died the work was still far from finished. His great-nephew, who was his heir, was created a baron in 1903 and took the title of Lord Armstrong of Cragside and Bamburgh. The 2nd baron still owns the castle, which is now open to the public.

Sad to relate, at close quarters, once inside the walls, magnificent and costly gesture as it may have been the restoration is unconvincing. The simple truth is that it has been overdone and Bamburgh is not much more than the Victorian idea of what such a castle should look like. Nothing can detract from the splendid commanding position and impressive outline, but the interior is disappointing.

The church at the opposite end of the village is far more worth seeing although easily missed when approaching from the east, so firmly does the castle dominate the scene. This is not over-restored out of all recognition. Although probably built on the site of a seventh-century Celtic and later Saxon church, no trace of these remains. It dates genuinely from the twelfth and thirteenth centuries, with particularly fine spacious proportions.

In a crypt under the church are buried members of the somewhat wild Forster family whom Lord Crewe saved from bankruptcy on marrying Dorothy Forster. Amongst these is General Thomas Forster, who was condemned to death for taking part in the rising of 1715. According to one account he was rescued from Newgate prison in London by his sister, niece of Lady Dorothy, who bribed the guards and had a copy of the key made by the local blacksmith. To ward off pursuit it was then announced that he had died and been buried at Bamburgh. A tombstone was inscribed and an empty coffin buried. When he finally died in 1738 the same stone was inscribed a second time. Unfortunately for the truth of the story, the tombstone only bears the one date.

Grace Darling, born in the village in 1815, is buried in a somewhat elaborate canopied tomb in the churchyard. In 1838, aged twenty-three, she rowed side by side with her elderly father, the keeper of the Longstone Rock lighthouse on the Farne Islands, to the rescue of a crew shipwrecked in a storm and in imminent danger of drowning. It was a particularly heroic feat since both knew that without help at the oars they could not themselves hope to return. Before the fame of her exploit had dimmed, she died of consumption, aged twenty-seven. Today there is still a Grace Darling Museum in Bamburgh, including amongst other relics the actual twenty-one-foot coble she helped to row.

Bamburgh is an attractive village, but a constant stream of visitors since the days of Grace Darling has undoubtedly affected it. Today it has most of the features of a professional tourist trap, from postcards and pottery to set teas and bed and breakfast. We were glad to move on down the coast.

The groups of cars parked at each open space in the sand dunes along the coastline and the overflowing litter bins testified to the nearness of Newcastle, only sixty miles away. Seahouses, the next small fishing town, is clearly geared to this tourist traffic. For all that it is a busy herring fishing port as well. The small harbour is full of life and movement with fishing boats moored side by side preparing for the sea and the quayside thronged with Northumberland holiday-makers whose gay clothes contrast strangely with the fishermen in their blue jerseys, turned-down thigh boots and battered nautical caps.

In the summer months daily trips can usually be made from here to the Farne Islands, the outermost extremity of the geological formation, the Great Whin Sill. There are twenty-eight of these scattered small islands, consisting of an inner and outer group and ranging from $1\frac{1}{2}$ to $4\frac{1}{2}$ miles off the coast. The largest of the inner group is known as Inner Farne, some sixteen acres in extent with cliffs eighty feet high. It was here that St. Cuthbert withdrew from the world. The largest of the outer group is known as Staple Rock, with three huge columns of rock sixty feet high at one end. The Longstone lighthouse is in this outer group.

Approached close-to by boat these islands appear much larger than one expected. There is a fascinating variety of bird life to observe: eider ducks, guillemots, razor-bills, puffins, shags and cormorants, to name only a few; but there is no doubt that the seals are the chief attraction, for the Farne Islands are the only breeding place of grey, or Atlantic, seals on the east coast. It is possible to watch them disporting themselves on the smaller rocky islets from quite close range, humping over the ground in ungainly fashion, but, once in the water, bobbing and diving with fascinating ease. Scarcely a spare patch of rock appears visible, at first, for the mass of delightful small youngsters, winsome females, large matrons and vast whiskery males who are the last to roll, grunting protestingly, off into the water as the boat finally draws too close.

The islands are owned by the National Trust and are administered by a committee composed of Trust members and members of a body known as the Farne Islands Association, formed originally with a view to protecting rare birds breeding there after the passing of the first Birds Protection Act in 1880. It is this committee which has been faced with deciding the vexed question of culling the seal community. Evidence that the seals had increased in numbers from around 1,000 before the war to over 3,000 and were affecting the livelihood of the inshore fishing community finally led to a number of youngsters being humanely culled. Controversy over this action has since raged bitterly.

Without involving myself either for or against this particular issue it must strike anyone as absurd that no action should be taken to protect our fishermen from the cut-throat competition of foreign trawlers. Already it is almost too late. Sweeping the North Sea with fine nets, which kill all sizes of fish, including young stock, they have almost denuded the fishing grounds. Creeping along the edge of the three-mile limit and often encroaching inside it, they have no interest, as our fishermen traditionally have had, in preserving the grounds for future fishing. From all over the Continent and as far as Russia, they are being allowed to ruin the future of what has always been one of the country's great staple industries. Unless the three-mile limit is very shortly extended to a five- or ten-mile limit, as has been done in Norway and Iceland, our fishing industry will be ruined and our supply of fish, on which we have always relied, will cease. In effect we are allowing the country to be robbed of one of its chief assets without protest and, compared with this, the seals on the Farne Islands are a small matter.

Not far beyond Seahouses is the rather fascinating old harbour of Beadnell (see pl. 11). This is the only east coast harbour which actually faces due west. It was owned at one time by Sir John Craster, who presented the lime kilns beside it to the National Trust and gave the harbour itself to the fishermen. Moored there are the old type of high-prowed coble for seine net fishing that have been in use for centuries.

Close to Beadnell are the 800 acres of Swinhoe estate, recently bought by the Duke of Roxburghe in an economic foray into Northumberland. It looks pleasant land in the coastal belt, but we did not have time to examine it closely. Nor did we have time to stop at the ruins of Dunstanburgh Castle, which we saw silhouetted against the skyline as we drove south, for we had an appointment at Craster Tower with Sir John Craster. A vigorous supporter of the inshore fishermen of the Northumbrian coast, he had opposed the abolition of drift netting for salmon on their behalf, but was overruled by the Hunter Committee. He had also advocated strongly the culling of the seals on the Farne Islands, on which subject I had read his letters to the papers with considerable interest.

We turned through the old archway behind Craster Tower.

It is part of an ancient fortification, for there have been Crasters at Craster since before the coming of the Normans. Sir John came forward to greet us. Greying, with a slight limp, dressed in a well-worn tweed shooting suit, he led us into a pleasant Georgian room and with more than Georgian hospitality, having enquired our tastes, poured us out Regency measures of whisky. I noticed that it was a clear malt whisky.

"This must be much the same as they use to make the mead liqueur on Holy Island," I remarked.

"Yes, it is. I've always drunk it. Good stuff. Of course, you know I'm chairman of the company," he replied. "Now, what do you want to know about the seals?"

"Well, I know you're vice-chairman of the Farne Islands Committee and I wanted to hear your views," I replied.

"Well, that's quite simple," he began. "My views are that the cull was absolutely necessary, and anyone in a position to know entirely agrees that this is so. It was carried out with complete humanity and I sincerely hope that all the screams of ignorant sentimentalists will not affect the planned programme of culling for the future. There can be no doubt that the inshore fishermen, who find it hard enough to make a living anyway, were suffering considerable losses from these seals."

At that moment he was called to the telephone. By the time he had returned we were feeling the mellowing effects of the whisky. We discussed field sports and natural history, both subjects in which he is greatly interested, as well as his views on drift netting and seals, ending up with the surprising success of his mead distillery on Holy Island. J.P., sportsman, shrewd business man and passionate champion of the rights of the Northumbrian fishermen, with whom his family has been associated for more than nine centuries, he was an entertaining and hospitable host.

We left with regret and drove on down past Alnmouth. In many ways this is to my mind the pleasantest of all the Northumbrian coastal towns. From a distance it consists of an attractive cluster of red-tiled and grey-slated roofs above colour-washed and brick houses perched on a small hillock above a tiny harbour formed by the estuary of the Aln. On investigation there appears to be little more than one unspoiled main street. Beyond lies a satisfactory stretch of sandy beach and the sea. For a simple holiday with no other requirements it would be hard to find a better small village by the sea, provided that the sun was shining.

Warkworth, beyond Alnmouth, has been an attractive old feudal town, but the fine once-fortified bridge by which it is entered is being superseded by a concrete structure. In the past Warkworth has known invasion by the Scots and a notable massacre was even perpetrated here in the twelfth century, when 300 people sheltering in the church were put to death by the Earl of Fife. As late as the fourteenth century, one of the Percies, in a letter to the king from Warkworth, mentioned dressing at midnight by the light of burning villages which had been pillaged and fired by the Scots. Today the invasion is from the south and the massacre is presumably being made in the name of progress, but it is none the less painful to witness.

The Norman church is worth a visit, if only for the notable length of the nave, possibly the longest in Northumberland. The castle, basically Norman, with later additions, was owned by the Percies from the fourteenth century onwards but was allowed to fall into ruin in the sixteenth century, when Shakespeare set some of the scenes of *Henry IV* there. The regular keeper was away on the day of our visit. We asked the dreamy-looking youth who had taken his place for the keys of the keep, giving access to the look-out tower, not normally open to the public. The view over the surrounding country is certainly outstanding.

A little-known treasure story* relates to Warkworth Castle. It seems that a previous keeper noted for his idle dreamy ways dreamed on three successive nights that if he dug beneath a

---

* For similar treasure story see pp. 128–9, *Soho for East Anglia*.

certain mound he would find a blue stone and beneath it a strangely shaped pot full of gold. He told a friend.

"Why don't you have a look?" asked his friend.

"I think I'll just wait and see if I dream it again tonight," the keeper temporised.

The night passed without the dream recurring, but in the morning there was a gaping newly dug hole where the mound had been. Beside it lay a blue stone exactly like the one in the keeper's dream and the remains of a shattered pot of strange shape. On making enquiries, the keeper learned that his friend had gone. Announcing that he had unexpectedly come into money, he had left the town that morning, never to be seen again. The blue stone may, however, still be seen in the ruins.

About a mile up the river below the castle on the opposite bank is a hermitage, which is well worth visiting if only for the journey by boat up and down this delightful stretch of the tree-lined river Coquet, famed for its trout and salmon fishing. We went to see it expecting nothing more than a typical eighteenth-century 'romantic' folly, but this proved to be a very different proposition, dating probably from the fourteenth century. Instead of a single chamber here was a small 'Swiss Family Robinson' residence literally carved out of a cliff face projecting over the Coquet.

A short walk from the landing place on the ground floor were the remains of a kitchen and hall. Up some stairs was the chapel with a vaulted ceiling impressively carved from the solid rock. There was also a rock-cut altar and a window with carved tracery, as well as the remains of other carving still visible. Beyond was a Sacristy and beyond that again a Solar, which must have been a pleasant room overlooking the Coquet. It seems there used to be access to the hermit's garden and orchard above, but the whole bears traces of weathering and vandalism.

Legend has it that a rather impetuous young knight, Sir Bertram, was to marry Lady Isabel of nearby Widdrington when she was carried off by a rival suitor. Owing to one of those knightly cases of mistaken identity, while attempting to rescue her from this rival, he slew her brother instead and as the maiden was attempting to draw his attention to the mistake she also received a mortal blow. It was said he built the chapel as an act of penance and spent the rest of his days there. Unfortunately the story has no basis in fact.

The first records of it date from 1487, when Thomas Barker was appointed "chaplain to celebrate mass in the chapel at a yearly stipend of 66s. and 8d.". In 1531 Sir George Lancastre, chaplain to the 6th Earl of Northumberland, was appointed to "myn armitage bilded in a rock of stone within my parke of Warkworth" with the pleasant emolument of twenty marks yearly, pasture for twelve cattle, one bull and two horses, also two loads of wood and a draught of fish every Sunday. It appears to have been a comfortable sinecure, which fell into decay after the Dissolution of the Monasteries.

We turned in and towards Brinkburn Priory on the other side of the Great North Road. On the way our attention was caught by what looked at first sight like a flying saucer already landed, or else a vast mushroom grown to Jack and the Beanstalk proportions. Approaching closer, by the simple expedient of driving over some grass fields, we found that it was an ultramodern type of water tower of streamlined concrete, no doubt offering less resistance to wind than conventional designs. Even so we would still not have been in the least surprised to see some little green men with antennae sprouting from their heads peeping over the edge at us.

While examining this erection, I gave the dogs a run in the open, bearing in mind the experience of a local man, Edward Cook of Togston, nearer the coast. He was a noted breeder of pointers in the nineteenth century and took one of his favourite dogs with him on a visit to the United States of America. To his distress he lost the dog near Baltimore. Some months later, to the amazement of his family, the dog turned up at its old home in Togston. When Edward Cook in due course returned he found the dog was there before him. Yet every attempt to find out how the dog had made the journey proved fruitless.

Crossing the Great North Road and the Wooler road beyond it, we arrived eventually by a devious route above the Coquet again. Brinkburn Priory Church, which is all that remains of the old priory, was recently given to the National Trust by the owner, Miss Fenwick, and was still undergoing repairs to the fabric, but we were kindly given the keys. We turned down a steep drive to the water's edge. There, unexpectedly, stands the priory church in the most perfect setting imaginable, within a fisherman's cast of the bend in the river.

Architecturally it is outstanding. Although only 130 feet in length, the Transitional Norman arches and the exceptional height of the roof give a graceful illusion of spaciousness and size worthy of a cathedral. On seeing this church one realises how magnificent some of the ecclesiastical ruins in the Borders must have been in their prime. Fortunately Brinkburn, though raided by the Scots, was not destroyed.

The story goes that a party of Scots raiders unable to find the priory were guided to it by the sound of the bells being rung in thanksgiving for their deliverance. After the raid it is said the Prior in disgust had the bells thrown into the Coquet. A similar story is related of Blanchland in County Durham, also Jedburgh, Melrose and Dryburgh over the Border.

The church fell into disrepair after the Dissolution, but was exceptionally well restored in 1856. The stones from the priory itself were used to build a rather uninteresting mansion house close by, which is now understandably deserted, for the setting, though beautiful, is undeniably damp. The discoloured patches creeping up the stones emphasise this point.

We continued alongside the Coquet to Cragside, the seat of that Lord Armstrong who decided at his breakfast table to buy Bamburgh. When he bought the steep hillside above Rothbury in 1863 it was almost barren. Today the grounds are famous for

their rhododendrons and azaleas. Terraced drives blasted in
solid rock lead through them, apparently endlessly, to the
moors above.

Before paying our entrance money and entering the grounds
we knew nothing of this. We intended merely to look at the
house and drive out again. Forty-five minutes later we were
still driving through overpowering walls of rhododendrons in
full bloom almost meeting above the car like a tunnel of
tropical foliage. I had every sympathy with the wretched hiker
perspiring under a heavy pack, whom we met at one point.

"How do you get out?" he panted despairingly.

At one point the drive leads through an archway actually
under the mansion house itself, so that for a brief period one
has the full benefit of Lord Armstrong's architectural eccen-
tricity, for it is obvious at a glance that the wretched architect,
Norman Shaw, was chivvied by his formidable client from
gable to turret. It is a curious hotchpotch of periods and styles
ranging from the Neo-Gothic and Stockbroker Tudor to the
honestly Victorian. The result, which defies logical description,
would not perhaps be out of place on an artificial Swiss Alp
in Hollywood.

The house is not open to the public, though it contains, I
gather, among some exceptional items of furniture a table said
to have been made out of the oaken piles of the Roman bridge
at Newcastle. In 1880 it was the first house in the country to be
lit by electricity, the power being provided by damming a
stream and forming a series of lakes on the hillside. The fact
that this was hideously inconvenient and frequently breaking down, does not seem to have disturbed the millionaire
owner.

When at last we found the exit gate in front of us, we drove
into Rothbury with a sigh of relief. Rothbury is the capital of
Coquetdale, a most attractive village and important sheep-
farming centre. In the days of Border reiving, Rothbury was
plagued by raids from the Scots and also from the unruly men

of Redesdale and Tyndale, but the inhabitants themselves had an almost unparalleled reputation for lawlessness, so they probably gave as good as they got. Its stone-built, slate-roofed houses snugly enclosed in a hollow above the Coquet, it is an unmistakeable Northumbrian Border village. There is an affinity with Scots architecture, but each is clearly and instantly distinguishable.

At this point my friend Selby undertook the map reading. We passed through Lorbottle, much raided by the Scots, now merely a hamlet. A ballad recording a raid in 1549 is extremely descriptive:

> Mark Ker rode, and Mark Ker rode on,
> But never a hoof or horn saw he,
> Till he came to the ford at Larbottle burn,
> Where a dainty drove lay in the lea.

As we drove on and on into the hills, feeling a little like Mark Ker, we discovered that we were destined for Biddlestone Hall, once the ancestral home of the Selbys. Unfortunately, when we arrived at the spot marked on the map it became apparent that the house had been demolished. Our map reader hastened to point out that he belonged to a different branch of the family, on the Holy Island, or coastal side.

Investigating the site, we found that only a chapel remained, once obviously incorporated in the house but perhaps of older origin. Underneath was an archway in which we subsequently learned there had been a well into which a hound of the West Percy had fallen when out hunting. It was discovered six weeks later, still alive, having survived by eating the carcase of a sheep which had also fallen into the trap. Understandably the hazard has now been filled in for safety.

We went on to Alwinton, where we discovered that our ancestor-hunting-by-proxy was not yet finished. We were led firmly into the church. It is rather unusual in that it is built on solid rock on two levels to suit the terrain. It also contains memorials to past Selbys. The time to visit Alwinton, however, is during the annual Border Shepherds' Show and Sports in October. Then this quiet corner of the Northumbrian hill country really comes alive.

CHAPTER 5

Alwinton to Langholm

Lock the door, Larriston, Lion of Liddesdale,
Lock the door, Lowther comes on;
  The Armstrongs are flying,
  The widows are crying,
The Castleton's burning, and Oliver's gone.
Lock the door, Larriston; High in the weather gleam
See how the Saxon plumes bob in the sky,
  Yeoman and Carbineer,
  Billman and Halberdier,
Fierce is the foray, and far is the cry.

JAMES HOGG, 1770–1835

THE ANNUAL Border Shepherds' Show at Alwinton is obviously an occasion looked forward to expectantly throughout the year by the shepherds and farmers, not to mention their wives and families, who live in the isolated hill hamlets and farmsteads of these windswept Cheviot hills. Its scope extends far beyond the immediate radius of Alwinton itself, which for the past hundred years has merely been the convenient centre. Supporters flock from Alnham, Harbottle, Holystone, Windyhaugh and Netherton, from Glanton, Whittingham and Rothbury, even from as far afield as Yetholm over the Border, or further. Marquees sprout in the Haugh where the show is held and from early morning there is a constant procession of Land Rovers, sheep lorries and cars on the narrow winding roads leading to it.

The programme is liable to bewilder anyone accustomed to

an agricultural show in the south—or even in the Scots Border country, though a similar show is held in Yetholm on the Saturday previous to this. In the spirit of friendliness noticeable on all sides it has perhaps an affinity to the Common Ridings which are a feature of the Scots annual Border celebrations. There is a tremendous and knowledgeable partisanship apparent, much of which will be lost on anyone who does not know the people or animals concerned. For this is primarily a show for animals and men, unlike agricultural shows, which are increasingly becoming merely a shop window for new machinery. To these hill men, sheep and working dogs—that is collies and terriers—come first. Hounds come a close second.

To start the day, there are sheepdog trials and to the uninitiated it might seem impossible that the dogs could answer so readily at such a distance, turning the sheep and guiding them, singling out one of their number apparently magically, in response to the merest inaudible whistle, or almost invisible gesture. The sheep themselves are judged in turn. Lambs, ewes, tups and gimmers, Cheviots and Blackfaces, they may all look much alike to those who do not make a living by them; but the eyes watching at the ringside as each entry takes its turn are as knowledgeable and critical as the judges' themselves.

A turn round the marquees provides plenty of interest. There is a formidable showing of flowers and vegetables and in the section presided over by the ladies there are quantities of eggs, butter, jams and jellies, as well as cakes, breads and scones, including such local items as 'Wholemeal Fadge' and 'Singing Hinneys', the former an unleavened bread and the latter a type of scone. In the bar close by the Northumbrian burr is very evident in the buzz of talk. Yet, according to the entries, there are plenty of good Border Scots names present: Scott, Graham, Armstrong and others. It is apparent the old Border rivalries have long been forgotten.

Meanwhile, the collies and terriers are judged and the foxhounds also have their turn, sterns waving gaily in the air; but the chief excitements of the afternoon are the sports, with a fell race, wrestling and hound trailing, as well as other items. The interesting point to a stranger perhaps is that the entrants for the fell race, some three miles of steep up and downhill running, and the competitors in the wrestling, Cumberland style, are not all by any means young men.

I mentioned fell racing to a friend of mine who had been brought up in the dales and he smiled reflectively.

"When I was a boy I used to be sent out on my pony to act as marker in the fell races and they used to have to run round me," he said. "What still sticks in my memory is the number of bald heads and grey hairs I always used to see well to the fore beating the young men."

To those who have never seen it, hound trailing, the last item of the day, is a strange sport. The principle is that the hounds are trained specially to follow a trail, which is usually laid in the shape of a rough circle of as much as ten miles ending up not far from the starting point. The aim, as with a point-to-point, is to have as much of the course in view as possible and the hounds are bred specially for the sport. They are much lighter than an ordinary foxhound, some forty pounds as against an average foxhound's seventy. They are trained on laid trails and work individually, not as a pack. It is a popular sport in Cumberland, especially with miners, and keen supporters will travel miles to enter their hound in a trail during the season from June to October. Betting on the results may be considerable.

The probability is that it is a variant of the old Elizabethan style of hunting. Then they enjoyed standing on a knoll listening to the sound of hounds hunting within the confines of a park, commenting as each in turn gave tongue. This may seem a strange static form of hunting today, conditioned as we are to following hounds across country, but to true hound lovers it has a very understandable fascination. The direct equivalent was until lately to be found in the coon-hounds and foxhounds of the Kentucky mountains where, over a barrel of home-brewed moonshine, the hunters listened to the hunt waxing and waning in the distance, naming each hound in turn and following the chase from the comfort of their verandah by sound alone.

The hounds are led to the starting line, for the most part plunging eagerly in front of their owners at full stretch of their leads. They are slipped at the starter's signal and bound off on the trail at full speed, giving tongue spasmodically. They are soon out of sight and the handlers then move slowly to the finishing line ready to encourage them when they come into view. As soon as they are seen, pandemonium breaks out as each handler strives to encourage his particular hound by shouting, whistling, waving caps and even towels, leaping up and down in their enthusiasm. Finally, as the winning hounds cross the line, the handlers are almost as exhausted as the animals themselves. For those involved, the excitement reaches a remarkable pitch. It is hardly possible not to be infected by it.

More clearly than any other way, such a day reveals the pattern of life in the hills. Some of these farms deep in the Cheviots, it must be remembered, are still liable to be cut off for weeks at a time in the winter as a matter of course. Such a life is deep-rooted and satisfying, but not for weaklings.

Returning to our journey, after leaving Alwinton we drove through Harbottle. All that remains of the Norman castle once owned by Robert de Umfraville is now a grass-covered mound prominent by the roadside. We did not stop to investigate it but went on to the rather charming little village of Holystone.

We parked the car in front of the pleasant small inn, the Salmon. A little way behind the inn across a grass field and concealed in a copse of trees is a spring known as the Lady's Well. Possibly once part of a Benedictine nunnery, which was sited where the church now stands, but looking more as if it might have been a Roman Bath before that, the spring is reputed to be the spot where Paulinus, that indefatigable

dunker of heathens, baptised 3,000 Northumbrians at Easter in
A.D. 627 (see pl. 12).

Oblong in shape, the bottom lined with quartz, the well, or
spring, is an attractive spectacle with the sun shining on it. In
the centre is a Celtic cross and on the bank a statue of Paulinus.
In spite of the vast number of hairy Northumbrian bodies he
immersed, a notice makes it clear that any such proceedings
would not be tolerated today. It reads:

"Water from this well is used as drinking water for the
village. Dogs and bathing not allowed."

From Holystone we took the road for Otterburn. This is the
site of the famous battle, renowned in the best known of the
Northumbrian ballads as Chevy Chase and in the Scots version
entitled the battle of Otterbourne. A bitter fight between
Douglas and Percy, the two rival champions of the Borders, it
resulted in the death of the Douglas and the capture of the
Percy, as well as considerable carnage on both sides.

According to *Chevy Chase*, one of the heroes of the day on
the English side was Squire Witherington, possibly some rela-
tion of that unfortunate Lady Isabel, whose death reputedly
caused the building of Warkworth hermitage. The ballad in-
forms us:

> For Witherington my heart was woe,
> That ever he slain should be;
> For when both his legs were hewn in two
> Yet he kneeled and fought on his knee.

We stopped at the inn, the Percy Arms, where we intended
to try the shooting they then advertised. This, we learned, was
on a moor a few miles south-west above the Tarset burn. We
found our way there with some difficulty because it soon became apparent that the moor had been completely planted up
with trees by the Forestry Commission. There was indeed no
longer any moor left unplanted.

Eventually we stopped and walked through plantations

about fifteen years old and ten feet high until we came to infant plantations only two or three feet high. Here we hoped to find and put up a few grouse or black game, but the results were disappointing. It was only as we turned to give up in disgust that the dogs suddenly acknowledged their first scent and came on point at the edge of a well-grown plantation. A covey of grouse was flushed amongst the trees and, firing amidst the branches rather like snap-shooting woodcock, we collected a right and left and a single bird, one of the oldest and hoariest cocks I ever remember seeing.

A hundred yards or so further on our way to the car we put up a fine young roe doe, which disappeared in a series of gliding bounds over the heather. Apart from that we saw disappointingly little life on what looked very much as if it had once been a fine sporting moor. Where we might have expected to find the scent, if not the sight, of black game there was no sign of anything at all. Of course it has often been asserted that the Forestry Commission's policy towards black game has been to turn a blind eye to deliberate out-of-season persecution, but I had hoped to see some proof to the contrary.

After this abortive grouse-shooting expedition we returned to the Percy Arms. The hallway appeared to be filled with dogs. There was a splendid large yellow labrador and an equally large black labrador accompanied by a fine flat-coated retriever. Behind them their owner, dressed in khaki shorts and tweed shooting coat, was obviously also just back from the moors, but somehow had remained immaculate without a hair out of place.

"Good-looking dogs. You don't often see them as big as that nowadays," I remarked to him.

At this the manager of the Percy Arms, who was hovering in the background, hastened to introduce me to Mr. Douglas Nicholson, the chairman of Vaux, the company that owns the inn and many others in the Border area. He is obviously a powerful personality and one of the few company chairmen I have met who could contrive to look dignified and perfectly capable of taking charge of a board meeting in shorts.

"I like the larger size of labrador," he said. "I always think it puts two years on their life."

This is not a popular opinion, but it happens to be one I subscribe to, as long as the owner has the time and the energy to exercise a larger dog adequately. The general tendency in this country is to breed gundogs too fine and too small. The results are weeds to be seen in all breeds. I said as much.

"I've just spent a couple of hours shooting a brace and a half of grouse in that forest you grace by the name of moor. I didn't think much of it," I added.

"On the moor we were on we only got two brace all day," he pointed out. "But suppose you show me on a map where you went."

I outlined the area and told him of the growth of the trees. It transpired that he had not visited this moor for nearly twenty years and he was perturbed to learn how much had been planted.

"At the end of the war I rented these moors on a ninety-nine-year lease," he explained. "Since then the Forestry Commission have taken the area over for planting, but if it is as bad as you say it is I feel I should have a case against them for damage to sporting rights."

"I'm sure you have," I agreed. "And I shall be most interested to learn what your lawyers think."

It says a considerable amount for Mr. Nicholson's attention to detail that he explored the area himself the following day while fishing in the Tarset burn and subsequently instructed his lawyers to sue the Forestry Commission. Bearing in mind Lord Iveagh's famous action against the Forestry Commission in East Anglia, when the Chairman of Guinness won his case, it is interesting to find the Chairman of Vaux opposed to them in the Borders. The juggernaut of the Forestry Commission has often ridden roughshod over individuals. It is well there should be those prepared to resist.

These enormous state forests, such as the 110 square miles of Kielder Forest, of which this erstwhile moor had become a part, inevitably alter the face and character of the countryside completely. The entire ecology of the land is changed. Such mass planting may be all very well when there is no other use for the land, but where it interferes with farming interests, or indeed with any other interests, it is questionable whether it is justifiable, either economically or as practical policy.

Just beyond where we were shooting the Duke of Northumberland has been carrying out an interesting experiment on his farm at Emblehope to prove that it is possible to combine forestry and farming successfully. On this farm since 1952 he has been planting shelter belts of about fifty acres of mixed plantations and running Cheviot sheep in conjunction with them. The results have already proved satisfactorily that sheep and forestry can be combined successfully and that there is no necessity for this policy of mass afforestation.

Sufficient good farming land is being swallowed up by concrete each year for us to weigh carefully how each acre is used today. With ever-increasing demand and continually decreasing land available sporting rights are also increasing enormously in value all the time. The Forestry Commission's aim too often appears to be a variant of Parkinson's Law that forestry expands to fill the space available. This is neither desirable nor sensible, however great a demand there may be for timber.

The rolling wastes of rough pasture and heather-covered moorland between Otterburn and Bellingham are true Border reiver's country. In the blue gloaming it would be no surprise to see a party of roughly attired Scots on shaggy ponies herding a flock of sheep, or a herd of cattle, basket-handled swords at their sides, or perhaps a Jedhart axe on its lengthy stave projecting like a lance over their shoulder as they rode. At the sight of this rolling countryside, deserted save for the sheep, any Borderer must feel a tingling and freshness in his blood; a stirring of atavistic tendencies. Here a horse seems the natural means of transport. It is the car which is the anachronism. I asked my companion what he felt about it.

"It's a wild bit of country, all right," he admitted.

We drove on into Bellingham in silence. On the fringe of Kielder Forest, it is a quiet small Northumbrian Border town, now almost doubled in size by the addition of some unimaginative Forestry Commission housing on the outskirts. We had a look at the church which was undergoing repairs. The solid stone slabs of the roof and the thick heavily buttressed walls indicated that it has been built like others on both sides of the Border with a view to defence. Close by, the new fire station and the gleaming fire engines indicated the greatest threat in this highly afforested area today.

We went on to have a quick look at Brown Rigg school on the outskirts of the town. The wooden huts on a rise by the roadside are not at first inspiring, but on closer inspection they are attractively laid out round a quadrangle and the idea seems an excellent one. It is an experimental boarding school run on public school lines by the Northumberland County Education Committee. There are three houses for boys and two for girls in the 13–15 age group. The parents pay 13s. 9d. a week towards their keep and the venture has been so successful that it is being copied elsewhere. As an alternative to raising the school-leaving age it might be feasible to extend such a scheme to those who would benefit from it.

From Bellingham we turned up the valley of the North Tyne which winds attractively amid the trees. The Robsons, who lived at Charlton in Tyndale, were well known as reivers. It was said of them that the lady of the house would serve her husband a spur on a covered platter whenever the larder was bare. Their most notorious exploit was after they had raided the Grahams of Netherby and driven off their sheep, which they then discovered had scab. This infected their own flock and so incensed them that they raided the Grahams again. This time they hanged seven Grahams with the warning that "neist time gentlemen cam to tak ther schepe, they were no to be scabbit".

This route leads through the centre of Kielder Forest. Originally started as far back as 1926 as a counter to unemployment on Tyneside, it has been vastly extended since 1940 and many of the trees have already grown to sizeable proportions. The name 'The Blackcock' for the inn at the small village at Falstone was scarcely appropriate for an area now so changed, More suitable might be 'The Roebuck'.

The Forestry Commission town of Kielder was as depressing as most such planned centres are liable to be. The newest part of it, with its school for 180 pupils of typical shoe-box architecture, might have been worse—as the older part proved—but it has all been laid out with a remarkable lack of imagination. Situated in a hollow in the hills the green monotony of the trees all round intensified the slight feeling of claustrophobia. To live here trees would indeed have to be your life. Kielder Castle itself, a nineteenth-century shooting box of no architectural merit, is now a working man's club for Forestry Commission workers.

It is only on seeing the enormous size of a forest such as this and the institutional treatment of their employees that one appreciates fully what a soulless giant monopoly the Forestry Commission has become. One begins also to appreciate the value of a body such as the Timber Growers' Organisation which protects the interests of private forestry owners against arbitrary actions by the Forestry Commission, notably in the matter of negotiating prices. It would appear that a little prompting from private enterprise is occasionally required to help the executives of the commission to distinguish the wood from the trees.

Driving out of the Northumberland National Park, out of the Forestry Commission area and over the Border into Scotland we finally entered Liddesdale. Turning south once more we were now close to the Larriston featured in the stirring ballad at the start of the chapter. It continues with a roll call of the English:

> Bewcastle brandishing high his proud scymitar,
> Ridley is riding his fleet-footed grey,
>> Hedley and Howard, there,
>> Wandale and Windermere,
> Lock the door, Larriston, hold them at bay.
> Why dost thou smile, noble Elliot of Larriston?
> Why does the joy-candle gleam in thine eye?
>> Thou bold border ranger,
>> Beware of thy danger,
> Thy foes are relentless, determined and nigh . . .

Then comes a roll call of the Scots:

> Little know'st thou of our moss-troopers' might;
>> Linhope and Sorby true,
>> Sundhope and Millburn too,
> Gentle in manner, but lions in fight.
> I have Mangerton, Ogilvie, Raeburn and Netherbie,
> Old Sim of Whitram and all his array,
>> Come all Northumberland,
>> Teesdale and Cumberland,
> Here at the Breeker Tower end shall the fray . . .

It ends triumphantly:

> Howard ah! woe to thy hopes of the day;
>> Hear the wild welkin rend,
>> While the Scots shouts ascend,
> Elliot of Larriston! Elliot for aye.

In the wild and lonely wastes of rough pastures amongst the mossy hags and rocky outcrops of Liddesdale these verses seem to fit perfectly. Anyone visiting Liddesdale for the first time should read them beforehand, preferably aloud. They capture the challenging nature of the countryside exactly.

Even if one knew nothing of the history of Hermitage Castle the very approach through Liddesdale would have been enough to make one expect something formidable. Even without being sensitive to atmosphere, a chilling perception of its lonely isolation, if nothing more, must be experienced at the sight of it. In the grey of an overcast day, desolate amid these barren wastes, it seems a grim, forbidding four-square pile standing sentinel in the pass.

Originally site of a hermit's dwelling, from which it takes its name, the castle built in the thirteenth century was early owned by the de Soulis family, followed by the Douglases and for a period, when captured by the English, by the Dacres. Regained by the Scots, Archibald 'Bell-the-Cat' Angus, being of doubtful loyalty, was ordered to exchange it for Bothwell Castle on the Clyde. Thus when the Earl of Bothwell was wounded in 1566 by the notorious reiver Jock Elliot he was brought here. Then it was that Queen Mary made her ill-advised journey to his bedside from Jedburgh, returning the same day, a distance of more than fifty miles on horseback over some of the wildest country in the Borders. At the end of the sixteenth century the castle passed to the Buccleuchs and in 1930 to the Ministry of Works.

A couple of hundred yards west of the castle above the Hermitage Water, near the ruins of the old chapel, is a grass-grown mound eleven feet long, the legendary Cout o' Kielder's grave. It has been suggested that this legendary knight of giant stature, who gained the nickname of 'Colt' of Kielder, may have been Sir Richard Knut of Kielder, who died around 1290. According to the legend he was drowned in the pool beyond his grave while trying to escape after the wicked Earl of Soulis, who was in league with the devil, had cast a spell over him.

The earl himself was reputed to have suffered an even more

unpleasant death at the hands of an outraged countryside, having been wrapped in lead and boiled alive on the nearby Nine Stane Rig. In fact he seems to have died in Dumbarton prison charged with treason. A further story connected with the castle but unsupported by evidence is that Sir Alexander Ramsay was deliberately starved to death in the dungeon by Sir William Douglas, but maintained himself alive for seventeen days on a trickle of corn from the granary above.

As ruined castles go, it is not a very satisfactory one, although it looks impressive enough at first sight. In 1820 the then Duke of Buccleuch restored it almost out of recognition. There now remains practically nothing to see inside the outer walls. Yet in spite of that and the fact that the Cout o' Kielder's grave has been opened and been found to be empty, and although the legends have no foundation in fact, there is a curiously disquieting atmosphere about the place. A visit there is to be recommended chiefly for the drive through Liddesdale to it.

It is only on looking at a map that one realises what a natural route Liddesdale was for English invasion. It is only then, too, that one realises how strategically Hermitage was placed to guard the entrance. Yet one can also see at a glance how freely the Border reivers would have been able to move around these hills, from Liddesdale through to Tyndale, or over Tarras Moss to Langholm and up Eskdale or Teviotdale. The very names begin to read like a ballad.

The most direct way to Langholm from Hermitage Castle is straight over the hills to Mosspaul and the views on this route are very fine; but we decided to go on to Newcastleton. A model village built by the Duke of Buccleuch in 1793 and originally intended as a weaving settlement, though now a sheep centre, it still retains a slightly planned appearance with a long main street and formal greens. From here we were tempted to take the minor road over Tarras Moss, which leads almost directly to Langholm, over extremely wild country, but we decided instead to make a detour into Cumberland and come round by Canonbie so that my friend, a keen fisherman, could see the Esk on the way.

Difficult road though it is, I was rather disappointed that he did not see Tarras Moss. It was here that the Earl of Bothwell, in close pursuit of Jock Elliot, fired and wounded him in the hip. Shortly afterwards he was himself bogged, whereupon the reiver turned and, in spite of his wound, attacked the Warden of the March and ran him through with his dagger. It was this wound which left Bothwell at death's door in Hermitage Castle and precipitated Mary's visit. It also inspired Jock Elliot's well-known verses:

> I vanquished the Queen's Lieutenant,
>   And gar'd his fierce troopers flee,
> My name is little Jock Elliot,
>   And wha daur meddle wi' me?

> I ride on my fleet-footed gray,
>   My sword hanging down by my knee,
> I ne'er was afraid of a foe,
>   And wha daur meddle wi' me?

It was supposedly when besieged in their stronghold in the centre of Tarras Moss by Sir William Carey, Warden of the English March, that a party of Armstrongs slipped away under cover of darkness over secret paths in the bog, raided his land and carried off some of his cattle. After returning safely they reputedly sent him one of his own cows with their compliments and the message that "fearing he might fall short of provisions during his visit to Scotland, they were sending him some English beef".

From Newcastleton we turned in the opposite direction to Tarras Moss and very soon crossed the Kershope Burn into Cumberland. On the hill above rises the green mass of Kershope Forest, contiguous to Kielder Forest in Northumberland, below runs the Liddel Water. It was here after one of the meetings of the Wardens of the Marches, when a day of truce was declared and disputes between both sides settled by arbitration, that a notorious Scots reiver, William Armstrong, better known as Kinmont Willie, was seized in violation of the truce by the English and imprisoned in Carlisle Castle. The famous ballad of Kinmont Willie recounts how "the bold Buccleuch" led a party of picked men to his rescue.

A little further on the left of the road stands Stonegarthside Hall. At first glance it appears a normal enough, quite attractive house of the seventeenth century with two wings and typically steep crow-stepped gables. Only on closer inspection does one appreciate that the central portion is unfinished. There is merely a curtain wall with empty window spaces and orna-mental battlements. The story goes that three brothers built it and, failing to agree on how it should be completed, left it unfinished.

We turned up towards Bewcastle Fell, which marks the northern boundaries of Cumberland. This hill area seems to have much in common with the Cheviots above Alwinton and bears exploration. But, being limited for time, we turned back and crossed the Liddel which marks the Border until it merges with the Esk below Canonbie. This part round Canonbie was once all known as the Debatable Land, since no one could decide whether it was Scots or English. It was here that the Grahams lived, whose brush with the Robsons of Tyndale has already been mentioned. With the Armstrongs and the Elliots in Liddesdale they were noted reivers on both sides of the Border.

According to the Rev. John Russel, writing in the *Statistical Account* of 1795 on the 'Parish of Canoby', serious agriculture was only introduced by Dr. Graham of Netherby, followed by the Duke of Buccleuch, in the latter half of the eighteenth century. He noted revealingly:

Many circumstances have occurred within these 20 or 30 years to introduce a change in the dispositions and manners of the people . . . Industry was not formerly the characteristic of this part of the border. Gambling . . . horse-racing and cock-fighting were much in vogue . . . As a check upon the conduct of the lower individuals, his Grace has reserved the cot-houses upon the farms in his own power; so that, at every term, any offender . . . can be turned out of the parish. In all the new leases a clause of nullity is inserted in case of moral delinquincies therein specified.

On the scenery he recorded:

The central part of the parish is intersected by the river Esk; and the post road from Edinburgh to London, by Langholm and Carlisle, passing in the same direction, through a line of venerable oaks, planted by the hand of Nature; and other trees of different descriptions, holds up in varied procession to the view of travellers, the most beautiful and picturesque scenery that is perhaps to be met with anywhere in Scotland.

The road from Canonbie to Langholm is still most attractive, the tree-lined Esk winding close beside it. The Rev. Russel wrote:

There is an abundance of fish after floods . . . They are catched by the long net, the rake net, the rod and sometimes killed, or rather murdered, by an instrument called a Lister. The lister is a shaft with 3 iron prongs barbed on one side, fixed on the end, not unlike the figure of Neptune's trident. With this the fish are struck, both when stationary and running in the shallow water; and the remarkable clearness of the water of Esk facilitates the execution of the bloody deed.

In a little book dated about 1790 entitled *A Tour from London to Elgin*, by a Mr. Willis, the author wrote of this stretch of the journey:

The whole way through the Duke of Buccleuch's plantations and woods to the next stage at Langholm is singularly picturesque. A more varied prospect I never saw, and rich throughout. At every mile the landscape shifts and you are presented with an entire new change of scene, the river Esk runs at your side through the whole.

On the subject of Langholm he went on:

Langholm is the first Scotch village you enter, and the change of manners, dress and character, strike most forcibly at once. It is scarce more violent at Dover and Calais, the people of either sex were in general without shoes or stockings with a kind of stole, they call a maud, over their shoulders and slung across like a sash. The men wore Highland bonnets and the women a singular cap most singularly disfiguring, called a mutch.

It is surprising how biased the English still were towards the Scots before Sir Walter Scott tinted their view with the rose colour of romance. Yet Langholm, it must be admitted, is different from the towns in Cumberland. Once larger than the neighbouring towns, hence known as 'The muckle toon o' Langholm', it was made a burgh in 1628. Though not large by present-day standards it is very much a Border town, set like most of them on a river, with several bridges in and around it, one of which Telford helped to build as an apprentice.

In another book* I once described it as "a sleepy rather charming small town". For the greater part of the year I see no reason to alter that description, but there can be no doubt that it does not apply during the Common Riding. Then is the time to visit Langholm.

These Common Ridings are a feature peculiar to the Scots Border towns and to understand the Borders properly they should be seen and experienced. A mixture of beating the bounds, a memorial service, a reunion of exiles, a pageant, a town sports, a steeplechase and a glorious binge, they vary from town to town and baffle description. Though most Border towns now have them those of Selkirk, Hawick and Langholm are the oldest.

The Langholm Common Riding developed from 1765 when the town crier, Archibald Beattie, was employed to check the town boundaries each year, a ceremony which he performed on

* *Soho for the Colonel.*

foot. After his death in 1816 the bounds were first ridden and thereafter the number of riders increased each year. Today the Langholm celebrations differ slightly from other Border towns in that these are the only ones to include hound trailing and wrestling, as at the Alwinton Border Shepherds' Show. Considering the proximity to Cumberland, where these are favourite sports, this is scarcely surprising.

The day starts at 5 a.m. with the flute band playing in the town. The hound trailing on the Whita Hill above the town follows. Then back in the town the town crier proclaims the Fair. The Cornet, the Langholm youth selected to carry the Burgh Flag, leads his followers on horseback and the day begins. The riding of the bounds by a youth selected from the town leading a procession of a hundred or more mounted followers is common to most Common Ridings, hence the name. In order to obtain a good view of the various ceremonies and also to learn exactly what is happening it is advisable to arrange for a local guide beforehand if possible, otherwise much will inevitably be missed.

It is typical of the lack of interest that the Borders undoubtedly has in tourists and tourism that these Common Ridings are not well advertised. On the whole, the Scots Borderer is immersed in the business of day-to-day living, whether it is rearing sheep, raising crops, or making tweed, or woollen garments. Much the same may be said of the Northumbrians. Off the well-beaten tracks there are simply no facilities for tourists. Although the Borderer has a tremendous pride in his own locality he has no particular desire to share it with others.

Unfortunately on the Scottish Tourist Board calendar the date of the Langholm Common Riding was inadvertently set down a day late. When we arrived post-haste from the Game Fair in the south, having travelled past Hadrian's Wall at dawn to reach Langholm by 5 a.m., it was only to find the streets filled with the litter of carnival and the town tight shut. Those few people to be seen in the streets had a distinctly dazed look.

93

On a subsequent occasion we drove into Langholm and called at an inn for refreshment and information. To begin with there was only one other customer present who at once engaged us in conversation. Soon noticing our interest in the town and my friend's English accent he deliberately broadened his own and enquired with humorous intent:

"What for are ye speirin'? D'ye ken what speirin' is?"

Fortunately he answered his own question and saved me quoting Burns on the subject of "a chiel amang ye takin' notes", but I could not let a statement about the Duke of Buccleuch pass unchallenged.

"He can walk from Gretna Green to Edinburgh, without going off his own ground. It was in the papers."

"Perhaps, a hundred years ago," I suggested.

"No. It was just a few months back in the Sunday papers."

I gave up the argument as there was clearly nothing to be gained by proving the inaccuracy of the statement and he was soon talking interestingly on the Common Riding. I thought he seemed exceptionally well-informed. Then a fresh arrival explained why. He had been town crier for nearly thirty years and the hub of the proceedings.

The newcomer was a medium-sized, powerfully built man. His muddy Wellingtons, overalls, cap and raincoat could belong nowhere but a farm.

"It'll be mainly black faced sheep hereabouts?" I queried.

"Aye, that's so."

"Have you been with sheep long?"

"I've been with sheep and cattle fifty-seven years and if I had my chance I'd do it again," he replied simply.

With his clear blue eyes and fresh complexion he was obviously thriving on it. In the course of further conversation it transpired that he was grieve on the nearby estate of Westerhall.

"Westerhall was owned by Sir Frederick Johnstone, who won the Derby twice," explained our first informant as soon as the name was mentioned. "Each year since whatever colours won the Derby have been taken as the town colours for the Common Riding."

As we turned to go eventually, he unexpectedly presented us each with a booklet, of which he seemed to carry a supply in his pocket. Imagining it was a tract of some kind (though not on Temperance) I started to thrust mine into my pocket, but my friend, quicker off the mark than I, opened his and read the title:

"*Langholm and Eskdale*, by John Elliot."

Once again quicker than I, he immediately enquired:

"Are you John Elliot?"

His guilt was obvious and we reciprocated the compliment by standing another round. Subsequently reading the booklet, I found it a comprehensive guide to Langholm and district, including an excellent description of the Common Riding, but at the time we were not allowed a respite from Mr. Elliot's unflagging quips. Even as we left he characteristically had the last word. Contemptuously eyeing the old dyed army greatcoat I was wearing he said:

"Next time ye come, remember that Langholm's a textile town and dinna wear a coat like yon."

CHAPTER 6

Langholm to Jedburgh

I've heard the lilting, at our ewe-milking,
Lasses a-lilting, before the dawn o' day;
But now they are moaning, on ilka green loaning,
The Flowers of the Forest are a' wede away.
We hear nae mair lilting at our ewe milking,
Women and bairns are heartless and wae;
Sighing and moaning on ilka green loaning-
The Flowers of the Forest are a' wede away.

JEAN ELLIOT

W RITING ON Langholm in 1793 in the *Statistical Account* the
Rev. Thomas Martin expressed strong views on the prohibi-
tion of whisky, painting an alarming picture of the effects of
over-indulgence and adding: "Beer is the natural and wholesome
beverage of the country." How far Mr. Elliot would agree
with him on this I am not sure, but in his excellent guide to
Langholm he endorsed the Rev. Martin's description:

The verdant hills beautifully skirted with wood, which
shelter it on the E. and W.; the Esk, 'o'erhung with woods',
gliding gently along, the town appearing through the inter-
vening trees and the hills and woods at a distance (assuming a
semicircular form) terminate this charming landscape; a landscape, of which, as containing an assemblage of rural beauty,
and romantick scenery, it baffles the happiest efforts of imagination to give an adequate description.

It is difficult to know which route to choose beyond Langholm. The road through Eskdale and Ettrick to Hawick has

some wonderful views and is strongly to be recommended, but as we were once again limited for time we chose the more direct road alongside the Ewes Water. In passing, it might be noted that this habit of calling a burn, or river, a water is an attractive one common to the Borders, as instanced by Liddel Water, Ewes Water and Gala Water, to mention but a few.

At one time there was a notable forest of Ettrick above the Ettrick Water at the top of Eskdale. In 1530 James V gathered an armed party, ostensibly for a month's hunting in Ettrick Forest, according to Lindsay of Pitscottie, the historian:

The second day of June the King past out of Edinburgh to the hunting, with many of the nobles and gentlemen of Scotland with him, to the number of twelve thousand men; and then past to Meggitland and hounded and hawked all the country and bounds; . . . he slew, in these bounds eighteen score of harts.

It was subsequently said that he also made a clean sweep of a number of Border reivers, hanging Cockburn of Henderland and Adam Scott of Tushielaw from their own castle gates. Legend in both cases is, however, contradicted by the facts, which were that both were hanged in Edinburgh before he set out on his expedition. It does appear beyond doubt, however, that it was on this occasion that he hanged the notorious reiver Johnnie Armstrong and his followers at Caerlanrig beside Teviothead.

The circumstances surrounding the incident are now shrouded in hearsay and legend. Either Armstrong thought it wise to submit himself to the king and hoped for a pardon, or else James promised him safe conduct and then played him false. Either way the ballad shows that popular opinion was not on James's side:

> The King he wrytes a luving letter,
>   With his ain hand sae tenderly,
> And he hath sent it to Johnnie Armstrang,
>   To cum and speik with him speedily.

Johnnie comes with his men:

> May I find grace, my sovereign liege,
> Grace for my loyal men and me?

But the king replies:

> Away, away, thou traitor strang!
> Out o' my sight soon may'st thou be!
> I grantit never a traitor's life,
> And now I'll not begin wi' thee.

Johnnie pleads for his life:

> Grant me my life, my liege, my king!
> And a brave gift I'll gie thee—
> All between heir and Newcastle town
> Sall pay their yearly rent to thee.

But the king refuses again and Johnnie replies:

> I have asked grace at a graceless face
> But there is nane for my men and me.

The ballad ends:

> John murdered was at Carlanrigg,
> And all his gallant companie;
> But Scotland's heart was ne'er sae wae,
> To see sae mony brave men die.

Lindsay of Pitscottie wrote: "Efter this hunting the king hangit Johnie Armstrong, Laird of Gilnockie, quhilk monie Scottish men heavily lamented, for he was ane doubit man and also guid a chieftain as ever was on the borderis of Scotlande or England." Legend persists that the trees on which the Armstrongs were hung withered and died and that none will grow in their place to this day.

All the Borders area is dotted with defensive peel towers, either in ruins and empty, or restored out of all recognition and still lived in, but sometimes apparently unchanged. Not far

from the road beyond Teviothead is Branxholm Tower, once
the principal seat of the Buccleuchs and still owned by them. It
was totally destroyed by the Scots in 1570 to prevent its capture by the English invaders under Lord Hunsdon. Scott
romanticised it in his *Lay of the Last Minstrel*. Wordsworth, on
seeing the present building, which has been renovated out of
recognition, wrote: "It looks better in your poem . . . the situation however is delightful."

Some three and half miles west of Hawick is Harden Hall,
another old tower, not so very changed. It was once famous as
the stronghold of Walter (Auld Wat) Scott, a noted reiver,
who in 1576 married Mary Scott, 'The Flower of Yarrow', her
dowry being 'man's and horse's meat for a year' in return for
the proceeds of the first 'moonlit night'.

Whenever the larder was bare the lady was said to have the
endearing habit similar to the Robsons of Charlton of presenting her husband with a pair of spurs on a platter as a pointed
reminder that it required replenishing. Reputedly another of
her methods of prodding her man into action was to order the
herdsman in her husband's hearing to attend to Harden's cow.
This would so affront him that he would at once lead his men
on a raid and return with a herd of English cattle, as she had
intended. From all accounts, however, he needed little prompting. Once, while driving off some cattle on a raid, he was seen
to eye a large haystack longingly and heard to say:

"Had ye but four feet ye'd not stand long there."

By the recognised law of the Borders, the 'Hot Trod', a
cattle raider might be pursued over the Border "with hue and
cry, with horse and hound", but if he retained the cattle for a
week and a day without detection they automatically became
his property. The peel at Harden with a view for miles around,
standing above a steep-sided glen, the Beef Tub, where the
cattle could be corralled, was ideal for a reiver.

The unexpected result of one raiding expedition is told in the
famous story of 'Muckle Mou'd Meg', or unkindly named

large-mouthed Margaret. The Scotts of Harden also owned
Oakwood Tower on the Ettrick and at that time there was a
feud between them and their neighbour Sir Gideon Murray of
Elibank Tower, whose estate was adjacent. It was William
Scott, Auld Wat's son, who was careless enough to run into an
ambush while driving off some of his neighbour's cattle. Captured thus in the act he was taken back to Elibank Tower
where Sir Gideon intended to hang him. Lady Murray, however, had other ideas.

"Would ye hang a braw young laird like yon, when ye've
three no-weel favoured daughters to marry?" she demanded.

Sir Gideon was at once struck by the good sense of this.

"Right," he said, turning to William Scott. "Which is it to
be? Will ye marry my eldest lass, muckle mou'd Meg, or will ye
hang from yon tree?"

Being a lad of some spirit, young Scott replied staunchly
that he would rather be hung any day, but, on the earnest intercession of that experienced and determined match-maker Lady
Murray, he was given three days to make up his mind. In that
interval 'Muckle Mou'd Meg', posing as a serving wench,
acted as messenger between the handsome young prisoner and
his aged mother, the 'Flower of Yarrow', thus endearing herself to him. At the last moment, when he still remained ob-
durate and set on the hanging, she revealed herself. To everyone's relief the obstinate young laird then accepted marriage as
an alternative and lived happily thereafter.

Sir Walter Scott's grandfather was descended from these
Scotts of Harden. He was known as 'Beardie', having sworn
never to shave until the Stuarts were restored to the throne of
Scotland. The present direct descendant of the Scotts of Harden
is Lord Polwarth, who still lives there.

The principal family of the Scotts was, and still is, the Buccleuchs. Their name supposedly originated in much the same
was as that of the Turnbulls, another famous Border family,
the first of whom was reputed literally to have thrown, or

"The golden cross on a 'field of azure'—carried at each Common Riding by 'Cornet', who must be an unmarried 'callant'." Hawick Common Riding (p. 104)

15. "The nave—the fine wheel window—and the Norman doorway beneath i
Jedburgh Abbey from the tower (p. 112)

'turned' a wild bull which threatened the life of the king out hunting. Similarly, the first Buccleuch was supposed to have been a Scott who, when the king's hounds cornered a buck in an inaccessible cleft, or cleugh, went in and brought it out over his shoulders. Hence 'Buck cleuch'.

Much of the history of the Borders is bound up with the rise and fall of the particular families in power. Thus the Douglases, Red and Black (so called from the colour of their hair and cast of countenance, but merely rival branches of the same family), were all-powerful until the latter half of the fifteenth century, being superseded by the Maxwells and they in turn by the Buccleuchs. By Elizabeth's reign the Kers and the Buccleuchs were the 'firebrands of the border', but as the Borders settled so these reiving families established themselves. Like the Kers of Cessford, the Buccleuchs were promoted from Lord Warden of the Marches to an earldom, though they might still say, if challenged to their title on land, like Percy in Northumberland, that they had won it 'by the sword'.

The subsequent history of the Buccleuchs is tied in with fortunate marriages and inheritances. When Monmouth, bastard son of Charles II, married Anne, heiress of the 2nd Earl of Buccleuch, the fortunes of the family were set. On Monmouth's execution in 1685, her son inherited the title of Duke of Buccleuch and Monmouth. The 3rd Duke, born in 1746, inherited the title and estates of the Duke of Queensberry, 'Old Q', through the female line, thus adding the extensive Douglas lands around Drumlanrig in Dumfriesshire to his already very considerable holdings in Ewesdale, Eskdale, Ettrick and Liddesdale—not to mention those in Selkirk and around Dalkeith. Then indeed the Dukes of Buccleuch could have walked from Gretna Green to Edinburgh without leaving their own ground.

As the measures taken by James V against the Armstrongs are still remembered and held against him in Ewesdale so the measures taken by the 3rd Duke of Buccleuch to improve his land, as quoted earlier from the *Statistical Account*, have left a lingering resentment and suspicion. Although no different to those used by the Duke of Roxburghe or any large landowner of the day, Border memories are long and narrowly parochial. The burghs were constantly fighting against any encroachment of their common lands and there is still ready opposition to any suspected ducal pressures, either to Roxburghe in Kelso, or to Buccleuch in Langholm, Hawick and elsewhere.

Hawick (pronounced Hoic) is today a busy manufacturing centre for knitwear and woollen garments and with over 17,000 inhabitants is the largest town in the Borders by a long way. Enquiring about Hawick, I was told at first merely that it was 'a good shopping centre'. It is that and a good deal more, for Hawick, like most of the Scots Border towns, is best seen in festival mood, more especially during the annual Common Riding (see pl. 14). Then it is evident that it retains in full measure the corporate spirit peculiar to the Border towns and little short of astounding to a stranger.

On that famous night of the False Alarm of 1803, when the beacons blazed their warning, the Volunteers of Hawick turned out to a man. Although the eligible age for service was from seventeen to fifty-five the roll of names included: "Thomas Dyce, preacher, above age yet willing to serve; Walter Grieve, under age yet willing to serve." All the way down Liddesdale the Armstrongs and Elliots, alarmed by a mounted bugler galloping wildly down the valley since the beacon was outside their view, tumbled out of bed in darkness. Though some rode more than twenty miles and forded the flooded Liddel Water all had reported by daylight. False Alarm though it may have been, they proved themselves as ready to fight as their fore-fathers.

The same spirit, allied to a determination not to be outdone, was noted by the Rev. Robert Gillan when he wrote with remarkable prevision in the *Statistical Account* of 1793: "Were it not for the disadvantages and difficulties they have to encounter, the spirit of the inhabitants of Hawick would raise it to the first station of manufacture in the south of Scotland."

In the *Statistical Account* of 1845, written by the Rev. J. A. Wallace, he included the song of Hawick. Since it breathes the spirit of the town and the Common Riding I have included it in full. Sung by the 'Teris', as Hawick townspeople designate themselves, after the obscure phrase in it 'Teribus and Teri-odin', this is liable to be heard at public dinners, at rugger matches, including the famous Border seven-a-sides, as well as at the Common Riding itself. As given by the Rev. Wallace it runs:

> We'll a' hie to the muir a-riding,
> Drumlanrig gave it for providing
> Our ancestors of martial order
> To drive the English off our border.
>
> At Flodden Field our fathers fought it
> And honour gained, though dear they bought it;
> At Teviot side they took this colour,
> A dear memorial of their valour.
>
> Though twice of old our town was burned,
> Yet twice the foeman back we turned,
> And ever should our rights be trod on,
> We'll face the foe to Teriodin.
>
> Up wi' Hawick, its rights and common,
> Up wi' a' the Border bowmen.
> Teribus and Teriodin,
> We are up to guard the common.

The song sums up some of the most eventful points in Hawick's history. Burned probably more than once by the invading English, in 1570 the townspeople burned it themselves rather than surrender it to the invaders. In a letter from Lord Hunsdon, the leader of the invading forces, to Sir William Cecil, dated 23rd April 1570, we read:

The next day we marched to Hawyke . . . Er we cam ther, the

ynhabytantes of the towne unthacht all theyr howsys and sett
the thache a fyre, so att our cumyng ther was suche a smoke, as
we were skant able to enter the twone; but cawsyng the same
to be quenchyd with water, and helpt with men's hands, we
yncamped theare all nyght, with such vyttels as we browght
with us. Apon Thursday, as they had burnt theyr thatche, we
burnt the hole town.

Like most of the flower of the Scots Border manhood, the
Hawick contingent was killed almost to a man at Flodden. The
following year, when Dacre and other English reivers were
still marauding the Scottish Borders, confident that no opposition was left, the Abbot of Hexham, noted for his freebooting
propensities, camped with an armed band at Hornshole, only
a couple of miles from Hawick. Two hundred of the youths, or
'callants', of the town, who had mostly been too young to fight
at Flodden, raided the camp. They captured the Abbot's
standard and set the English to flight. The golden cross on a
'field of azure' borne back to the town in triumph, has remained
its banner ever since. A replica is carried at each Common
Riding by the 'Cornet', who must be an unmarried 'callant'.
The list of cornets goes back to 1703.

The celebrations at Hawick last a full week each year, the
dates being decided by reference to the pre-1752 calendar, but
falling in the first fortnight of June. They combine a reunion of
exiles with the riding of the Marches and end with a ball. Although the 'Cornet' has his 'Lass', the ridings are a solely male
affair. The stirring chorus of the 'Teribus' occurs frequently,
sung with all the emotion and rousing fervour of something
between the Eton boating song and a Maori war chant. If the
mysterious phrase 'Tyribus ye Tyriodin' can seriously be translated as an ancient invocation to the pagan Gods 'May Thor
and Odin keep us', descended in some strange way from a
Danish war chant, it would not be out of keeping.

We drove down the main street to the outstanding monument at the far end. A statue in bronze of a young 'callant' on

horseback bearing the captured colours triumphantly in one hand, it is strangely moving. By a local man, Major W. Beattie, it was unveiled by Lady Jean Scott in 1914 to commemorate the victory at Hornshole 300 years previously and the dead of Flodden. How ironic was the timing. By 1918 the sculptor himself was dead and in the interval more Hawick men had been killed than ever died at Flodden.

It was early closing day and the shops were shut, but the pavements were still thronged and a queue stood at the bus stop opposite the statue. On the other side of the road a group of modern 'ton-up callants' sat astride their motor cycles. As the sun tipped the statue of the young man on his prancing steed the present-day youth of Hawick leaped cowboy fashion aboard their machines and departed up the high street with a roar of exhausts and a chorus of wolf whistles. It was somehow symbolic. Hawick is a forward-looking town, very much alive, with a considerable future in front of it. Its roots may be solidly buried in the past, but it can still rely on its youth for the years ahead.

Taking the Jedburgh road out of Hawick, we decided to follow a circuitous route rather than the direct one. Two miles out of Hawick, my companion drew my attention to a simple stone memorial, a pillar topped by a circle with a carved cross and the date 1514. On the pedestal are the words: "Lest we forget". A few yards further on was a bridge. This we realised must be Hornshole where the 'Callants' of Hawick so successfully routed the Abbot of Hexham's men and captured the banner.

A little further on is the small village of Denholm. It consists of a large village green and just enough houses to go round it. It is chiefly noteworthy as the birthplace of the balladist and Orientalist Dr. John Leyden. Born here in 1775, a shepherd's son, he must have had a remarkable brain and ability, for he was entirely self-educated. He taught himself Latin and Greek before he was nineteen and appears to have been able to learn any new language in a matter of weeks. He died in India, aged thirty-six.

During the night of the Great False Alarm it was a tailor of Denholm who was heard moaning:

"Oh, mither. Ah wush ah wuz a wumman."

Beyond Denholm in Minto House at the foot of Minto Crags lived Jean Elliot, daughter of Sir Gilbert Elliot, who, it is said, bet her that she could not write a ballad about Flodden. She thereupon sat down and produced the song which for sheer feeling and beauty is amongst the finest in our language. Though most people know the first and the last verses given at the start of this chapter, fewer people seem to know the two centre verses, which for contrast always seem to me even finer.

At bucht, in the morning, nae blythe lads are scorning,
  The lasses are lonely, and dowie, and wae,
Nae daffing, nae gabbing, but sighing and sabbing,
  Ilk ane lifts her leglen and hies her away.

Dule and wae to the order, sent our lads to the border,
  The English, for aince, by guile won the day;
The Flowers of the Forest, that fought aye the foremost,
  The prime o' our land, are cauld in the clay.

We turned down the Rule Water past the small hamlet of Bedrule, once the home of the Turnbulls, amongst the un-ruliest of reivers in their day. On the outstanding conical peak of Ruberslaw, the Covenanters frequently took shelter from persecution. The rocky summit apparently provided plenty of hiding places as well as suitable sites for sermons, one rock being named Peden's Pulpit, after Alexander Peden, a noted preacher. On one occasion he was said to have been only just saved from capture by the dragoons, owing to the sudden descent of a providential and typical mist, which shrouded the summit.

I was glad to be able to entice my companion past it on the plea that we were short of time. He has an innate desire to climb any challenging-looking hills but I had no wish to climb some 1,400 feet for a close view of low-lying cloud. On a clear day I should imagine the views are superb and worth the effort.

Our next objective was the Border line at Carter Bar. Here, at Catcleuch Shin, was the meeting place for the Wardens of the Middle Marches. It was here that the Wardens of each side met on a day of truce to decide the claims and disputes outstanding between Englishman and Scot. In effect it was an informal court where, with a little give and take between the Wardens, the various issues could readily enough be settled. When, as often happened, the Wardens failed to agree, it could as easily result in a general mêlée since there was usually a considerable body of armed Borderers on both sides ready, as ever, for a fight.

In 1575 the Wardens were Sir John Carmichael, on the Scots side, and Sir John Forster for the English. The ballad of the event starts off, like all good journalese, a mixture of true report and drama.

> The seventh day of July, suith to say,
>   At the Redeswire the tryst was set;
> Our Wardens they affixed the day,
>   And as they promised so they met.
> Alas, that day I'll ne'er forget.

The ballad goes on to read like a roll call of the readiest fighters on both sides. On the Scots side were Armstrongs, Elliots, Douglases, Turnbulls, Cranstons and Scotts, while on the English side there were Fenwicks, Russels, Herons, Collingwoods, Shaftoes and Robsons. One can readily picture the scene with the two armed sides each grouped fairly tensely behind their leaders while the negotiations were in progress. Behind the Scots numbers of pedlars and hucksters were setting up their tents and stalls in anticipation of making the most of the crowds once the proceedings were over.

On this occasion matters did not go smoothly. Harsh words

were exchanged on the subject of one Robson, a Tyndale horse thief. Blows were exchanged and in no time a wholesale fight was in progress. The English, with the advantage of the hill, were pressing the Scots hard when the temptation of loot from the pedlars' stalls proved too much for many of them. At this moment, as their attack was losing its impetus there was the familiar war-cry of 'Jethart's Here!' and welcome reinforcements from Jedburgh armed with the formidable long-shafted Jedhart axes, arrived to turn the tables for the Scots.

> Bauld Rutherford he was fou stout,
> Wi' a' his nine sons him about,
> He led the toun o' Jedburgh out
> All bravely fought that day.

In a few minutes the English were on the run and the day was won. The 'Fray of the Redeswire' is of interest particularly as the last large-scale fight between English and Scots. In 1603 the Crowns were to be united, but it would be another full hundred years before the Borders began to settle down and a further half-century or more before settled agriculture began to produce the modern way of life we know today.

From Carter Bar there is a splendid view over the rolling foothills of the Cheviots on the one side with Ruberslaw and Minto Crags conspicuous on the other. Between lies the road into Scotland taken by the invading Tudor forces under first of all the Earl of Surrey in 1523 and then later under Lord Evers and the Earl of Hertford in 1544 and 1548. Then Jedburgh and all the towns and countryside as far as the Merse were ruthlessly burned and destroyed twice over. Then Henry VIII's orders "put men, women and children to fire and sword without exception when any resistance shall be made against you" were obeyed to the letter, leaving a legacy of hatred.

We drove down past Edgerston and into the foothills of the Cheviots. At one point we drove along the Roman road of Dere Street, now incorporated in the modern road, before descending to the small hill village of Oxnam. Here the attractive small whitewashed church caught our attention. We stopped outside and went to investigate it.

Outside still hangs an example of the 'jougs', that monstrous method employed by the Kirk Session during the eighteenth century for punishing the backslider, whereby the culprit would have to stand chained by the neck in an iron collar during the service. It was only finally suspended towards the end of the eighteenth century when one unfortunate was found hanged after the service, having apparently fainted during the waiting period. At one time common outside every church, there are now only a few examples still to be seen.

We went in search of the manse. A rather charming eighteenth-century white house nearby looked the most likely building. We approached hesitantly. A red-haired youngish man in an open-necked shirt was mowing the lawn vigorously. I enquired whether he knew where we could obtain the keys of the church. Since my encounter with a sporting horologist at Polwarth I was prepared for any reply.

"Oh, do you want to see my church?" he enquired, in rather surprised tones. "I'll be delighted to show you, certainly."

The personal pronoun did not escape me, but this alert slightly built young man with a disarmingly shy manner did not fit my preconceived picture of a minister in a hill parish. Somehow I had anticipated someone elderly, slow and ponderous with a Scots pulpit voice and intonation, given perhaps to pronouncements about lambing and providing weekly doses of fire and brimstone for his flock.

"Tell me, by the way," I enquired. "Why is it that Scots churches always seem to be locked, whereas English ones are always open?"

"Well, of course, you realise I can't speak for the English churches," he replied, with a smile. "But in the church of Scotland, we don't feel the idea should be encouraged that the only place we can pray to God is in church. We want people to realise that they can pray to God at any time in any place. Therefore we keep the church locked unless we are actually holding a meeting or a service there."

"Doesn't that simply encourage people only to pray when they come to church on Sunday?" I enquired.

I received a very direct look, but there was a humorous twinkle in his eyes as he replied:

"We try to make it plain that is not desirable either."

Although I had already begun to revise my preconceived opinions on Scots clergy I was to do so even more when we were shown inside the church. The pews of plain scraped wood, the plain glass arched windows looking out over the hills, and the complete simplicity of it was like a breath of fresh air after the many stifling over-varnished Victorian interiors I had seen. I said as much.

"I'm glad you like it. I do too," he said gravely. "But I had quite a job convincing my elders in the Presbytery meeting that it would look better this way."

Once again I noticed a twinkle in his eye and it occurred to me that the people of this hill parish had made a very sound choice of minister.

My friend drew my attention to a memorial tablet on the wall. It was the only one. It read:

This tablet is erected by CHARLES PHILIP DE AINSLIE, General in Her Majesty's army, Colonel of the 1st, or Royal Regiment of Dragoons, and member of the Royal Company of Archers, Queen's Body Guard, Nineteenth and last male representative of the family of that name, who for 310 years, possessed the tower and lands of Dolphingston in this parish, which by the marriage of his ancestress, Marjorie de Ainslie, passed into the family of Ker of Cessford in 1502, after a direct male descent of more than 700 years during which they were famous in their generations and had inter-married with most of the families of note in the south of Scotland, the name of De Ainslie expires with him who placed this record to the memory of an ancient race.

"I rather like that," my friend remarked, after studying it at length. "Even if he had to write it himself he was going to make sure he had a good epitaph, but because he wrote it himself there isn't a date when he died, so we're none the wiser."

Having seen and admired the church, the minister, Mr. Thompson, invited us to have tea with him in the manse. Over an excellent tea provided by his charming wife, we were introduced to his four young children. On learning that I was contemplating a book on the Borders he at once recommended consulting the *Statistical Accounts*. It transpired that he had himself provided material for the third in the series, which has recently been produced.

It is both pleasant and refreshing to meet a 'man of God', who is simply and sincerely that and is at the same time able to discuss a wide range of interests with discernment and humour. Mr. Thompson manages to achieve the unusual feat of being human and also of quietly radiating sincerity and conviction. I have met the combination before but it is unfortunately a rare thing. We left eventually reflecting that the parishes concerned are fortunate in their minister and his wife.

We drove towards Jedburgh, passing above the Jed Water within sight of Ferniehurst Castle, the erstwhile stronghold of the Kers of Ferniehurst, the rival branch of the Kers to those at Cessford. Noted for their left-handedness, the name Ker became synonymous with this trait and to the Scots to be Ker-handed, or 'Corrie-fisted', was to be left-handed. So pronounced was this that the spiral stairs in Ferniehurst Castle were at one time built with the opposite turn to the normal so that the Kers retreating up them fighting, sword in hand, would be at an advantage. Now much restored, after being frequently destroyed, the castle is a Youth Hostel. The Kers of Ferniehurst achieved the title of Marquis of Lothian and their family seat is now Monteviot House near Ancrum, beyond Jedburgh.

The approach to Jedburgh from the south lies past the ruins of the abbey. Originally founded in the twelfth century, it was destroyed no less than seven times between 1300 and 1545 by various English raids. It is only amazing how much remains. Compared with the other Scots Border abbeys a great deal survives although naturally of a variety of periods.

Investigating the ruins with my friend after arriving in Jedburgh on the day of the Common Riding ceremonies, we found the door to the spiral staircase in the tower was open. Climbing upwards we eventually reached the top of the tower, which is a fifteenth-century addition. The view would have been impressive had it not been for the slight drizzle falling. Below us, in the Haugh, above the winding waters of the Jed, the mounted sports following the Common Riding were taking place wholeheartedly in spite of the rain. The twin walls of the nave stretched beneath us, the south wall remarkably out of straight as seen from above (see pl. 15). At the other end of the nave and well below us, the fine wheel window stood out in detail. We were impressed and a little shaken by the sight of people looking like ants as they passed through the Norman doorway beneath it.

It was only when we finally turned to go down that we each realised that neither of us had any head for heights. The broken steps leading downwards without a guard rail were difficult enough for me. My friend, encumbered by an umbrella which he had insisted on carrying, as well as various parcels, found it almost suicidal. I was not surprised to learn, on a subsequent visit, that the stairs to the turret had been closed pending the installation of a safety rail.

The castle, which stood above the abbey, was completely destroyed by the raiders. It was rebuilt subsequently as the County Gaol. Now no longer used for this purpose, it appears to be a scrap merchant's dump. Much more worth visiting is the so-called Queen Mary's House, where Queen Mary lodged when ill in Jedburgh after her hectic day's ride to Bothwell's bedside in Hermitage. It incorporates part of an old bastel house, or fortified place of refuge for the population, a feature much required in Border towns. They were usually built in groups of three to support each other. This is apparently the only one surviving out of six in Jedburgh. It is now a museum.

Being right in the path of any invader from the south, inevitably Jedburgh suffered most and bore the brunt of many attacks. Yet Jedburgh men, with their dreaded double-edged long-handled 'Jedhart Axe' and their war-cry 'Jedhart's Here!', were famous fighters and to be found in the forefront of almost every skirmish or battle. Nor were they lacking on the night of the famous False Alarm when every Volunteer was found present save one, a lame tailor. For all that it was reported that one Jedburgh man with his wife and family took to the hills at once with enough food for a fortnight. The lesson of the past was still deeply ingrained.

The company drawn up before Lord Minto must have looked dashing in their uniform consisting of blue swallow-tailed coat with scarlet facings, white waistcoat and breeches, white cotton stockings and short black gaiters with a tall bearskin cap topped with a feather. Thus the appearance in the ranks of a man in working clothes with an old wheel-lock gun must have been particularly noticeable.

"Hullo, my lad, where are you from?" asked Lord Minto.

"Frae Horsley Hill, my lord."

"And, pray, where are you going?"

"To have a day's blattering at the French, my lord."

"But you're not a Volunteer."

"Mebbe no, but I'm willing to be one."

"Hold up your hand then," capitulated Lord Minto, and the latest recruit was sworn in.

Jedburgh has certain unique features, not least the considerable number of ways in which the name can be spelled; Jedworth, Jedburgh, Jedhart, Jeddart and many more. It is famous also for Jedhart Justice, which was the principle of hang them first and try them afterwards. The Jedhart axes already mentioned were peculiar to the town, as was the war-cry 'Jedhart's Here!' Two other not so well known features are Jedhart Pears, a small sweet variety of pear, and Jedhart Snails, a treacly sweet in the form of a snail.

In passing it is of interest to note that several of the Scottish Border towns seem to have a sweet tooth. There are for instance the 'Original Berwick Cockles', a striped peppermint-flavoured ball, also 'Hawick Balls', a type of treacle ball, as well as Jedhart Snails. Nor must one forget Selkirk Bannocks, a special variety of fruit loaf. It is probable also that the green boiled sweets known as 'Soor Plooms' are associated with Galashiels, for this is the town motto, commemorating an occasion when English invaders were surprised in a plum orchard and massacred.

At one time Jedburgh was famous for its witches. Today perhaps its most unique feature of all is the special game played annually in the streets, called 'Uppies and Doonies'. (A form of handball, with similar origins, is played in Denholm and Duns, see pl. 2.) When this game is being played it looks as if a riot had hit the town. All the shops have thick wooden shutters across their windows and traffic is liable to be held up for lengthy periods.

Although the rules are almost as obscure as those of the Eton Wall Game they appear to be something as follows: To start with, those born in one end of the town, the top end, are the Uppies, and those born in the lower end, are the Doonies. There are two goal areas in the opposing ends of the town. A number of balls, each about the size of a hockey ball, are thrown into the air and the game begins. Balls may be passed, kicked, or thrown, hidden on the person, in clothing or carried in full view. Players may go through buildings if doors are open and are not held responsible for any breakages that may be incurred. Tackling and scrimmaging amount to a free for all with no holds barred. When a ball is carried into the opposing goal area it is nicked with a knife.

This is the time when Jedburgh really celebrates, rather than during the Common Riding, which is comparatively quiet compared with many Border towns. I was explaining this to my friend and another very obvious Englishman whom we had encountered during the Common Riding ceremony. Dressed in a bowler hat and business suit, he had been attending a business conference and was on his way back to Newcastle when his car was held up by the procession. Stopping to watch, he had asked us what it was all about. I had done my best to explain both that and the game of Uppies and Doonies. I pointed out that with the advent of the new maternity hospital at the top of the town the Uppies must in due course inevitably outnumber the Doonies.

"Of course you realise that the whole thing originates from the time they cut off Englishmen's heads and used them as balls in the streets," I added.

"You're joking," said our new acquaintance.

"No, I'm not," I assured him.

I quoted M. de Beaugue, a Frenchman, who was with the French troops in 1549 sent to aid the Scots. He wrote of the treatment of an English prisoner:

They tied his hands and feet and head together and placed him thus trussed in the middle of an open space and ran upon him with their lances, armed as they were and on horseback . . . until he was dead and his body hacked in a thousand pieces, which they divided among them and carried away on the iron points of their spears. I cannot greatly praise the Scots for this practice, but the truth is the English tyrannised over the Borders in a most barbarous manner and I think it was but fair to repay them, as the saying goes, in their own coin.

"The English had a habit of raping any young girls and killing any old women who fell into their hands," I added. "So you see they did a lot worse than kick a few heads around. They were a barbarous bunch on both sides in those days."

115

But our new acquaintance was no longer listening. I could see he would never get over it.

"Damned savages, that's all. Imagine doing a thing like that. Kicking Englishmen's heads around. And still at it. I mean to say."

6. "The 'Braw Lad' of Galashiels—dips his standard in silent salute to the dead."
Galashiels Common Riding (p. 122)

7. "In the centre of a glorious horseshoe bend in the Tweed." Dryburgh Abbey,
from a print *c.* 1770 (p. 119)

18. "Attending the annual open-air service in the ruins." Melrose Abbey (p. 121

19. "It straggles from pepperpot-tower to battlement and crow-stepped gab
in a series of architectural hiccups." Abbotsford (p. 124)

CHAPTER 7

Jedburgh to St. Mary's Loch

Fair Maiden Lilliard lies under this stane;
Little was her stature, but muckle was her fame;
Upon the English loons she laid mony thumps,
And when her legs were cutted off, she fought upon her stumps.

TRADITIONAL

IT MAY be largely the dominating effect of the abbey ruins, but somehow Jedburgh, in spite of its many burnings, still gives the impression of being the most mediaeval of all the Scots Border towns. It is certainly not a town for heavy traffic. The procession of riders clattering up the narrow main street during the Common Riding seems absolutely in keeping with the surroundings.

We drove on towards St. Boswells. On the way we passed close to Ancrum, the scene of yet another battle, during which the English were defeated and their commander, Sir Ralph Evers, killed. The legendary 'Maiden Lilliard', noted above, was supposedly present, but the verse bears a close resemblance to that about the unfortunate Squire Witherington at the battle of Otterburn.

A cricket match was in progress on the large green at St. Boswells, opposite the kennels of the Duke of Buccleuch's hunt. My friend insisted on stopping.

"I didn't know they played cricket in Scotland," he commented.

I suggested that it was largely confined to the Borders and was merely another excuse to get to grips with the English. At

I   117

that moment we overheard a player's advice to the ingoing batsman:

"Gang in there, Wullie, and bat the hell out of them."

"Hardly what one expects to hear at Lords," was my companion's shocked comment.

In St. Boswells during the first half of the nineteenth century lived John Younger, a sporting cobbler and author, one of the first to describe in detail modern methods of fly fishing for salmon on the Tweed and an outstanding homespun character in an age of originals. Born in 1785, his family hailed originally from Haggerston in Northumberland. Though intended for the ministry he was forced by circumstances to follow his father's trade in St. Boswells.

Tall and powerfully built, he seems to have been as famed for his fishing, his fly tying and his literary abilities as he was for his cobbling. His business methods, however, appear to have been unusual. He refused to sell the leather thigh boots he made, which were entirely waterproof, under the then remarkably high price of five guineas, as he argued that the honest work that went into them was worth the price and that anyone who could afford them could afford to pay it.

He was a Volunteer at the time of the famous False Alarm and wrote of it:

There was Hume Castle with all the other signal hills in flames. Here was the signal summoning every man to his musket and all the village was soon astir, something between a hum and an uproar . . . We had not yet got our coarse regimental red coats, white breeks with black legs like Highland sheep, and so, of course, we marched as we were, in our various-coloured raggery.

He grew furious at the mention of William Scrope, Sir Walter Scott's sporting friend, who wrote *Days and Nights of Salmon Fishing on the Tweed* in 1845. It was unfortunate, to say the least, that this happened to include a description and plates of precisely the same flies mentioned already by John Younger in an article entitled "River Angling". In a book of the same name published subsequently he wrote wrathfully: "I described these flies numerically, 1st, 2nd, 3rd, 4th, 5th, adding a 6th as a favourite variation of my first. Mr. Scrope some year or two thereafter published a splendid book on fishing . . . Scrope's six flies *are mine*."

Sir Walter Scott he deplored as a man who "devoted a mind of considerable ability to the building for himself a monumental house and a name out of materials ferreted amongst the dirty rubbish of a very few late ages—three fourths of the whole, of course, a mere low bagatelle of literary flummery".

John Younger, the old radical, died aged seventy-eight in 1863. He had lived to see the rent of the fishing on the Mertoun beat of the Tweed trebled in price from five pounds to fifteen. During his lifetime, also, the stagecoach gave way to steam. By the time of his death the railway age was coming into its own and a network of lines was expanding throughout the country.

Newtown St. Boswells a mile or so beyond St. Boswells itself owes its existence to this change. It is merely a railway junction and centre, the Crewe of the Borders. If the rail cuts at present planned are put into effect it will no doubt soon be silent and deserted, but this is not a countryside where the people take kindly to being considered just so many convenient economic units. The weakness of economics, Adam Smith's revenge on the English, is that human nature cannot be satisfactorily equated in terms of a mathematical formula. The greatest mistake any business can make, including the nationalised industries, is to employ economists instead of accountants, or to pay too much heed to either. The Borderers still retain far too much individuality to put up readily with predetermined planning of this nature.

From St. Boswells we turned aside to Dryburgh Abbey, joining the main stream of cars and buses, for this is right in the centre of the well-trodden tourist track. It has to be admitted that the site of the abbey, in the centre of a glorious horseshoe bend in the Tweed, was particularly well chosen. Built in the twelfth century and knocked down finally by Lord Hertford in 1544, the ruins have their own charm as well (see pl. 17), but the chief attraction is probably the graves of Sir Walter Scott and the Haig family, which are in the precincts of the abbey.

We had a brief and unsuccessful interlude on a very sunny day fishing this beautiful stretch of the Tweed. It belongs to Mr. John B. Cormack, prominent Edinburgh business man and sportsman, owner of Dryburgh House, which is charmingly placed beyond the ruins. This house and the ruins were at one time owned by the Erskine family, who acquired them from the Haliburtons. There is an absurd eighteenth-century anecdote connected with a part of the grounds still known as Lady Haliburton's bower:

It is a circle of holly trees with a yew in the centre and has been used as a place to smoke tobacco in, to keep the house free from that noxious weed. Lady Haliburton was taken with a fit in this bower being overpowered with the fumes of tobacco—in taking her up one of the female servants thought she was dead and proposed to take her to the *dead-room*—the lady hearing what was said and not being able to speak, to let it be known that she was still alive, bit this maid in the arm with so powerful a hold that she hollowed out lustily.

From Dryburgh we drove on past the splendidly defensive tower of Bemersyde, which dates from 1535. The estate is still owned by Earl Haig, just as Thomas the Rhymer daringly prophesied it would be in the thirteenth century, when tenures were only liable to be measured in decades not centuries. The prophecy since then has scarcely ever been quoted in the same form twice, but at least its meaning is clear beyond doubt:

> Tyde what may betyde,
> There'll aye be a Haig in Bemersyde.

Turning up the hill beyond Bemersyde we arrived at the

famous stopping place above the Tweed known as Sir Walter
Scott's view. His carriage horses were accustomed to stop here
each day while he admired his favourite view. Here they stopped
firmly of their own accord for one last time when harnessed to
the hearse conveying his body to Dryburgh. High above a
wooded bend in the Tweed the view towards the peaks of the
Eildons is indeed a splendid one.

Being now on the regular tourist route, we had no difficulty
in finding our way to Melrose, which is the next accepted stop
on the normal itinerary of those 'doing' the Borders. It is an
attractive and surprisingly unspoiled little town, considering
that one of its principal industries undoubtedly is tourism. The
abbey ruins are the attraction. Of them Scott wrote, as the
opening lines to the *Lay of the Last Minstrel*:

> If thou wouldst view fair Melrose aright,
> Go visit it by the pale moonlight.

The fact that it is almost certain Scott never did anything of
the sort himself is by the way. This indifferent couplet was
enough to send visitors flocking to the ruins. Though few were
likely to remember much more of the poem the first lines were
easy enough. Hence Melrose's popularity since, to which the
crowds attending the annual open-air service in the ruins bear
witness (pl. 18).

Though Scott thus, almost accidentally, publicised Melrose,
it is not the finest of the abbey ruins. There are, admittedly, two
splendid windows remaining, but it is not as well preserved as
Jedburgh, nor as splendidly sited as Dryburgh. It must, to my
mind, rank third amongst the ruined Border abbeys. Kelso, at
one time probably the finest of them all, now comes at the
bottom of the list.

Melrose has one little-known custom. Each bride married
there is expected to kick a beribboned rugger ball into the
midst of a group waiting in the Market Place. The first aim is
to secure one of the ribbons for luck. Thereafter follows a

scrimmage for the ball until someone gets clean away with it. If it can then be safely hidden for three days it becomes the property of the successful contestant. During these somewhat rowdy proceedings in the streets of the town the police carefully turn a blind eye, as during the game of 'Uppies and Doonies' in Jedburgh.

"It'd be as much as our lives are worth to interfere," one policeman told me frankly.

It is only four miles from Melrose to its much larger neighbour, Galashiels, the largest of the industrial Border towns after Hawick. The mills and smoking factory chimneys are very apparent, but in the square in the centre of the town, the War Memorial suddenly makes one aware that this too is a Border town with a proud history behind it. Seeing the mounted figure of a Border reiver, lance at rest on his shoulder, sword by his side, the horse just reined back on to its haunches in an arresting pose, one is conscious at once of the green hills on either side and the curve of the Tweed close at hand. Behind is a ninety-foot reconstruction of a peel tower acting as the Burgh Buildings. Together the two make up an inspired memorial.

During the annual celebration of the Common Riding (see pl. 16), when the 'Braw Lad' of Galashiels on horseback faces the bronze equestrian statue and dips his standard in silent salute to the dead, it is a moment moving enough to affect the most cynical. The dead, not just of two world wars, but from Flodden onwards, the utter waste and futility of war, are brought most poignantly to mind. The Scots have indeed a genius for expressing their sorrow in song, in sculpture and in ceremonial.

In the crowd round the square during this ceremony I temporarily lost touch with my friend. I found myself outside an inn. It was packed with seething humanity, but I felt in need of a drink after this emotional catharsis. I forced my way to the bar and thus indirectly learned for the first time that 'Eck' is short for Alec, as it was here that I met Eck and Spud. Eck was short and square. Spud was enormous and rugged. They were obviously old friends from as far back as the 1914–18 war. They too had obviously felt the need for a drink after the ceremony and equally obviously it was not their first. Eck generously tried to sum it all up for me:

"Ye ken, it's kind of eemotional, that's what it is."

He turned to Spud for confirmation.

"Is that no what it is, Spud?"

"Aye, that's so," agreed Spud.

When I turned to go in a few minutes both shook me warmly by the hand and wished me well 'auld freend'. It would be easy to attribute this entirely to alcohol, but on these occasions the friendliness to be found in these Border towns has positively to be seen and experienced to be believed. In such company I would not have it otherwise. Large or small, dark or fair, invariably knobbly and usually weatherbeaten, whether he works in a mill or on the hill, the Borderer today is still a tough-looking specimen. The modern product is not so very different from his Border reiving ancestors.

On a subsequent visit to Galashiels I learned that this friendliness and communal spirit, so noticeable in these Border towns, is particularly marked here. There is a flourishing music festival held annually and a fifteenth-century mansion, Old Gala House, for four centuries seat of the lairds of Gala, is now an Arts Centre. There are also numerous societies and clubs, varying from a well-run dramatic society to a Borders Gun Club, who were misguided enough to invite me to give a lecture. I was interested to see what a complete cross-section of the town and its environs the members of this club provided. This, I feel, is typical of these Border towns. However large, they are still completely integrated with the surrounding countryside.

It is worth mentioning in passing that the word tweed originated from a mistake made by an English correspondent doing business with a Galashiels manufacturer. The latter wrote, offering tweel, or woollen fabric. The Englishman, knowing the river Tweed was somewhere near Galashiels, took it for granted the word was tweed and answered accordingly.

From Galashiels we followed the Gala Water back to the main tourist route and drove to Abbotsford, the home Sir Walter Scott built himself above the Tweed. John Younger described it as "monumental". Ruskin's description of it was: "Perhaps the most incongruous pile that gentlemanly modernism ever designed." Viewing it today it is staggering to learn that when Scott first bought the small and tumbledown farmhouse of Clarty, known locally as 'Clarty Hole', which stood on the site, he actually wrote: "My present intention is to have only two spare rooms, with dressing rooms, each of which, at a pinch will have a couch bed."

Scott's greatest difficulty was obviously controlling his own imagination. Once he had chosen the name 'Abbotsford' from the ford over the Tweed in front of the house, through which the 'Gala' Common Riders splash their way, the rest naturally followed. At first glance it is clear that this house was never planned systematically, but grew up step-by-step piecemeal as each romantic novel or epic poem yielded its golden harvest. It is the natural do-it-yourself, turret-by-turret product of this highly popular nineteenth-century author's success. It straggles from pepperpot tower to battlement and crow-stepped gable in a series of architectural hiccups (see pl. 19).

It is difficult now to realise what a resounding success Scott was in his day. He was a popular best seller not only in his lifetime, but also throughout most of Victoria's long reign. In spite of many adverse critics, he appealed to the public taste. He combined the historic with the romantic wrapped up in a dose of morality, which disarmed the censorious, and threw in some high-toned blood and thunder for good measure. The result was that he could command as much as £19,000 advance on a book and from £5,000 to £10,000 was commonplace. It is understandable therefore that in ten years more than £100,000 went into the building of Abbotsford.

No one would question Scott's good intentions. As Sheriff of Selkirk, local laird and sportsman, generous host holding open house, he was an extremely popular and attractive figure. Unfortunately Scott the man cannot be entirely divorced from Scott the romantic author. He did not exaggerate the Borders scene, but he had no hesitation in transposing events and places to suit his purpose, thus adding even greater confusion to the already chaotic Borders history. Whether the so-called 'mantle of romance' he cast over the Borders was entirely desirable is therefore, I feel, open to question.

One glance at his house proves that Scott was no architect. Nor was he a business man. He was in partnership with his publishers, the Ballantyne brothers, whom he had known since his Kelso schooldays. It seemed a happy arrangement until they went bankrupt to the tune of £117,000 and Scott was left to face the debts at the age of fifty-five. Admittedly his creditors were extremely gentlemanly and did not press the bankruptcy proceedings. He was allowed to keep Abbotsford, but he swore to pay off his debts and within six years he had written himself into his grave. Yet already, in that short time, he had earned the fantastic sum of £87,000.

Whatever one may feel about Scott's work, or his tastes in architecture, no one can deny his ability or pertinacity as a writer. Every professional writer must salute the sheer drudgery and hard slogging involved in rising as he did each morning at four or five and writing with a quill pen by gaslight. After lunch at 1.0 p.m., he regarded the afternoon as 'his own'. One has only to compare the Chantrey bust sculpted in 1820, the mouth firm and humorous, with the death mask in an alcove off his study, deeply lined and melancholy, to appreciate the killing pace he set himself. No knightly feat of which he wrote in his romances ever equalled such sustained effort.

I visited Abbotsford twice with different companions to see whether it affected me in the same way and to note their reactions. In building it, Scott was consciously or unconsciously creating a working background for the sort of book he wrote. He deliberately surrounded himself with historical curiosities which would excite his imagination. Wildly dissociated fragments of history such as a lock of Prince Charlie's hair, a model of Bruce's skull, Montrose's sword, suits of armour, battle axes, and similar oddments of romantic bric-à-brac fill the rooms. His desk, untouched since his death, still stands in his study surrounded by some of the 20,000 books of his library, also apparently untouched and no longer used.

Instead of a home and a workplace the house, or that end of it he used, has been converted into a literary shrine. It is all so very personal, so very much one man's creation, that there is a feeling of invading the author's privacy from the moment of entering his study. The suggestion that nothing has been altered since Scott's death is deliberately cultivated and even the clothes he wore are included as part of the peepshow. There is an indignity about thus laying bare the inner workings of his life and exposing his private background which rather appalled me. Possibly this feeling of desecrating a grave, or tramping through a mortuary in hobnailed boots, was accentuated by the jostling crowds of curious spectators, most of whom looked as if they had never read a word of Scott in their lives. I was interested to find that both my friends were similarly affected.

It is only fair to add that this is clearly a minority opinion. There are usually buses in the car park outside. There is a discreet brick-built tea room just inside the walls, chiefly I suspect for the benefit of the bus drivers. There always seem to be queues at the side door waiting to pay their entrance fee. Inside on trestle tables are heaps of souvenirs, tweeds and pottery for the tourist. Perhaps a notice on the wall at the turning to the stairs sums it all up best:

"Visitors are requested not to take eatables or ice cream upstairs."

One of Scott's most pleasing traits undoubtedly was a strong sense of humour. Once over the first shock of seeing his old home under present-day conditions he would probably have laughed. It is ironic that the author's best-selling work today should be this piece of stone romanticism.

We drove on round to the foot of the Eildons above Bowden Moor. From Mrs. Williams of nearby Huntlyburn House, which overlooks the moor, I heard a pleasantly innocuous ghost story. When she and her husband were moving into the house during the very dry summer of 1959 there were often workmen busy about the place until late in the evening. One evening about eleven two of the men, one being a particularly matter-of-fact cockney, saw a lengthy column of Roman legionaries marching through the gloaming over the moor. Being British workmen in the best tradition, they refused to allow a matter of serried ranks of Roman soldiery to interrupt their cigarette break. They continued to smoke and watch the column filing steadily across the moor for some five minutes or more. Finally it proved too much even for them. They switched their car headlights on to the moor and the legionaries faded from sight.

I told this story to my friend beneath the Eildons. I pointed out that it was not unreasonable since there was a Roman camp on one of them, the Trimontium of those days. I also pointed out that King Arthur and his entire Round Table were buried beneath them according to Cymbric legend. He was not interested. He had the bit in his teeth and was intent on climbing a hill.

"Before I started this book I didn't even realise that King Arthur was so strongly associated with the Borders, did you?" I enquired.

"No, I didn't. Now let's climb that hill in the middle," he replied singlemindedly.

"You realise that according to legend there was only one hill there before the famous Border wizard Michael Scott clove it in three, don't you?" I prevaricated.

"Come on," he replied, over his shoulder.

I could see he regarded them as too much of a challenge, so I gave up arguing. Instead I slipped on a pair of gym shoes and started over the heather after him. In heavy hobnailed boots he was soon slipping back one pace for every two he took forward. Anticipating that he might find the Eildons at close quarters too much to resist I had duly taken unkind precautions. I was thus able to admire the splendid view from the top for some time before he joined me. Although there is a direction indicator, it is advisable to take a pair of binoculars. The Roman camp on the neighbouring hill is not visible, but there is a tremendous field of vision across to the Cheviots and over the Merse to the sea, as well as in the direction of St. Mary's Loch. It must have been a splendidly defensive position.

After taking it more gently on the downward journey, although it is really not much of a climb, we reached the car and drove on towards Selkirk. Approached from this angle, or indeed any direction except from across the Ettrick Water it is not easy to realise how strangely Selkirk is placed on the side of the hill above the river. With its small triangular square and high street, Selkirk gives the appearance of a smaller town than it is, though nothing like the size of Galashiels or Hawick. Now a mill town like them, it was once famed for its shoemaking and the 'Souters', or shoemakers, of Selkirk have a long and proud history. They have also an intimate connection with Scott who was Sheriff from 1799 to his death in 1832.

It has been suggested that the Selkirk custom of 'licking the birse' required of each person becoming a burgess may have originated in Scott's fertile imagination. By this supposedly ancient ceremony three or four boar's bristles, such as shoemakers use, are dipped in wine. They are then passed through the lips of the prospective burgess before being affixed to the seal of his burgess ticket.

Selkirk's Common Riding, however, is acknowledged to be the oldest of all, reputedly dating back to the time of Flodden, when, it is said, only one survivor, named Fletcher, returned

with a captured English colour. Thus the dramatic part of the
ceremony here is when the Standard Bearer casts the colours
in the Market Square in front of the Flodden Memorial. In
connection with their Common Riding and with most town
occasions the 'Souters of Selkirk' have a song almost as popular
with them as the 'Teribus' in Hawick. It runs:

> Up wi' the Souters o' Selkirk,
>   And doun wi' the Earl o' Home!
> And up wi' a' the braw lads
>   That sew the single-soled shoon.
>
> Fye upon yellow and yellow,
>   And fye upon yellow and green!
> But up wi' the true blue and scarlet,
>   And up wi' the single-soled shoon.
>
> Up wi' the Souters o' Selkirk,
>   For they are both trusty and leal!
> And up wi' the men o' the Forest,
>   And doon wi' the Merse to the deil.

In 1791 the Rev. Thomas Robertson, writing in the *Statistical
Account* on Selkirk, wrote of this song:

Some have very falsely attributed this song to Flodden.
There was no Earl of Hume at that time, nor was this song
composed until long after. It arose from a bett betwixt the
Philiphaugh and Hume families; the souters (or shoemakers) of
Selkirk against the men of Hume, at a match of football, in
which the souters of Selkirk completely gained, and afterwards
perpetuated their victory in that song.

After the False Alarm of 1803, the Earl of Home of the day
called upon the contingent of 'Souters' to sing this song. "He
called in vain, and so sang the song himself, was rapturously
received, and at once enrolled a Souter." His descendant, Sir
Alec Douglas-Home, while still 14th Earl, early in 1963, was
made a burgess of Selkirk, duly 'licking the birse' and thus

being also enrolled a 'Souter'. He does not, however, appear to have sung the song.

Perhaps the most charming story of the False Alarm was the reaction of Lord Napier's butler: Mr. Pringle of Whytbank, captain of the troop of Selkirk Yeomanry, was visiting Lord Napier at Wilton Lodge, near Hawick, that evening. The well-trained butler entered the room and solemnly announced:

"My Lord, supper is on the table and the beacon is blazing."

With delightfully responsive decorum, Lord Napier re-marked:

"Whytbank, if the beacon's blazing, little supper may suffice. The sooner we ride to Selkirk the better."

Only one man in Selkirk failed to report for duty. Another tailor, Gideon Scott by name. There seems to have been some-thing about the tailoring profession which failed to breed heroism. Anyway Gideon Scott seems to have suffered for it.

On the return of the Volunteers to Selkirk they were paraded at the Market Cross in a hollow square, with the unhappy man in the centre. The Duke of Buccleuch, their Commander in Chief . . . said he was exceedingly sorry that any person in Ettrick Forest who bore the ancient and honourable name of Scott, should have disgraced it in such a cowardly manner. The buttons and facings of the tailor's uniform were then torn off, he was expelled from the company and drummed home.

On the road out of Selkirk the cauld across the Ettrick is worth watching when the salmon are running up it in a spate, dark shadows and gleaming silver shapes, leaping, fighting, thrusting ever onwards and upwards to the spawning beds. Beyond, on the far side of the Ettrick, is the plain of Philiphaugh where Montrose's Royalist forces were surprised over their camp fires in the morning and slaughtered by the Covenanting troops under General Leslie. Warned too late in Selkirk, where he had spent the night, Montrose attempted to lead a counter-attack with a hundred of his men. When that failed he wished to die on the battlefield, but was persuaded to save himself to fight again for his king.

It was close by on Carterhaugh that the football matches took place, such as already mentioned between the men of Selkirk and the men of Home. Another notable one watched by Scott and Hogg was between the men of Yarrow and the men of Ettrick. No small affairs these, but a hundred men or more a side, and frequently 'a close and stubborn struggle of more than three hours'. Football is still taken seriously in the Borders but not on quite such a heroic scale. It was probably during such a game that the old chestnut of Border rugger games was born, when the ball was punted out of the ground and a voice from the scrum was heard to say:

"Never mind the ball, get on with the game."

We drove on from there to the Duke of Buccleuch's estate at Bowhill, where we obtained permission from the estate office to visit Newark Tower in the grounds. Well-kept woods, trim hedges and verges and neatly ordered cottages indicated sound estate management. Bowhill itself was enlarged during the nineteenth century and is one of the Duke's principal seats.

The people of Selkirk are on friendly terms with their ducal neighbour and in 1963, along with the then Earl of Home, he was elected a 'Souter' after duly 'licking the birse'. They have never been easily overawed, as two stories illustrate which might belong to the last century or this. Characteristically, both relate to hunting, for this is still primarily a hunting country. The first concerns a disgruntled latter-day John Younger, who watched the ducal horse and rider galloping after hounds and remarked:

"Yonder's a thoosand poonds awa' chasin' hauf a croon."

On another occasion the Duke had a gate opened for him by a labourer during a time of unemployment. It was obvious the man was following hounds on foot. The Duke paused to thank him and thinking perhaps to help him added:

"Have you not got any employment?"

131

"I'm like yersel', yer Grace, I aye like a day's hunting."

We followed the signposts through fine pheasant coverts, which indicated the likelihood of some excellent high birds in season. Finally we came in sight of Newark Tower. It was here that after Philiphaugh in 1645 the Covenanters slaughtered the unarmed prisoners taken at the battle while a minister of the kirk commented: "The wark gangs bonnily on." The slope where the victims were buried is still known as 'The Slain Men's Lea'. It was to this tower, with its grim history, that Anna, Duchess of Monmouth and Buccleuch, retired with her children in 1685 after her husband's execution. In 1791 the Rev. Thomas Robertson wrote of it poetically in the *Statistical Account*: "Upon a peninsula, cut out by the surrounding stream, in the middle of this fantastically wild scene of grandeur and beauty, stands the castle of Newark, whose only inhabitants now are the mopping owl and chattering daw."

Unfortunately, in the early nineteenth century a factor of the Duke of Buccleuch knocked down the 'barmkin' walls; the outer walls inside which the cattle were driven for protection. He also used some of the best stones to build a farmhouse and other buildings on 'The Slain Men's Lea'. The 5th Duke of Buccleuch, he who restored Hermitage beyond recognition, insisted on the farmhouse being torn down and the stones replaced as they had been. The door of the ruin was locked and we did not feel disposed to go in search of the key, or return to the factor's office for it. A downpour of rain and the lack of a roof to the building convinced us that we had seen enough. We took the 'mopping owl' on trust.

We drove back past Selkirk, perched on its hillside along-side the Ettrick Water, and then beside the Tweed towards Innerleithen. This is a dull little roadside mill town, beautifully placed on the Tweed, but making the worst of it. We stopped for a chat with a head keeper whose house is tucked away below the Moorfoot Hills. On several occasions in the past ten years he has captured well-grown young eagles alive in his cage

10. "With the look of an old French chateau." Traquair House, near Peeble (p. 135)

11. "Beneath the Eildons—was a Roman camp." View from a distance (p. 127

traps. His worst pest would appear to be the picnicker who lights fires, or allows his ill-disciplined dog to roam amongst young birds. It was noticeable here that by the roadside a single plain wire fence had been erected, not to keep animals in, but to keep cars from parking on the verge. Otherwise this road, I was told, became completely blocked with parked cars.

We drove on into Peebles, a pleasant town with a broad main street, lying in a basin in the hills above the Tweed. Associated with John Buchan and his sister O. Douglas, who lived here, it has been fortunate in lying out of the way of any major routes north or south, so that it has developed peacefully throughout most of the Border upsets which affected the towns further east. It is a Border town, but with an unusual air of tranquillity. It has today rather the atmosphere of valetudinarian contentment that I suspect Moffat may have had when it was a popular spa in the eighteenth century. Peebles with its 'Hydropathic' is acknowledged to be the place for a rest cure.

It seems that at one time Peebles had a rather different reputation. In the *Gazetteer of Scotland* for 1845 the three salmon on the Peebles coat of arms were recorded as having "entered into the social language of the inhabitants, and at length brought matters to such a pass that it is hardly possible for any party however small to separate without *three* bottles, or measures of whatever liquor they may be drinking".

According to the records of the Tweeddale Shooting Club it was formed "at Peebles the second day of September, One Thousand seven hundred and ninety years". It subsequently embraced coursing as well as shooting. Although not the oldest club in the country for coursing it is undoubtedly the oldest shooting club in existence. It is notable also that in the list of original members was 'James Wolfe Murray, Advocate, Sheriff of the County'. Today the chairman is Lt.-Colonel Malcolm Wolfe Murray, his direct descendant. The records read like a roll call of famous Border names. The club still meets three times a year to dine, at the start of the grouse season, at the start of the partridge season and at the start of the pheasant season, in the same inn, the Tontine, in Peebles.

This seems a pleasant, civilised custom, whereas the Tontine, the custom after which the inn was named, was not. It was an arrangement whereby subscribers to a Tontine, who might be of any age, agreed that the last alive should have the sum subscribed. In the instance after which the inn was named the sum was £4,000 used to build the inn itself. Due to the encouragement it gave to murder, the custom was declared illegal during the nineteenth century.

Taking the southern road, we drove back the way we had come along the other bank of the Tweed. The scenery of the Tweed valley is best seen here from this side, with the rolling green hills and heather-clad slopes on either side of the river flowing silver and majestic, holding out to fishermen the promise of salmon at each bend and pool. This is part of the Peebles Association Water and much fished. Colonel Ryan described to me graphically how he and a water bailiff, heavily disguised as fishermen, once joined the rows of sportsmen standing almost shoulder to shoulder on the banks, many of whom were spinning with heavy triangular hooks in an effort to foul hook salmon. On that occasion to his disgust and everyone's surprise the only fish caught was a sea trout, quite legally. Association Water or not, it still looks extremely promising.

We stopped at Traquair House. It is approached from the back as the main gates are tightly shut and have not been opened since the eighteenth century. One story, and the most likely one, is that they were shut in 1796 when the 7th Earl of Traquair locked them behind the funeral procession taking his wife to be buried, declaring that they should never be opened again until a Countess of Traquair passed through them. As his son, the 8th earl and sole heir to the title, died unmarried in 1861, there has never been another countess. On the death of the 8th earl's sister, who lived to be nearly a hundred, the estate passed to the Maxwell Stuarts of Nithsdale. Mr. Maxwell Stuart subscribes to the more popular story concerning the gates, attributable to the romantic imagination of Scott, that they were closed after a visit by Prince Charles in 1745 and that the earl then declared that they would never be opened until a Stuart sat on the throne.

We approached the house with some interest. On dubious grounds it is claimed to be the oldest inhabited house in Scotland, but the present building is chiefly of the seventeenth century, incorporating a much older peel tower. The 1st Earl of Traquair, who built it, altered the course of the Tweed, at that time flowing past the house, in order to prevent the foundations being undermined. Though something may have been lost thereby it is unquestionably a most attractive house with the look of an old French chateau (see pl. 20).

The young man who showed us round turned out to be just down from Cambridge on a vacation job. From his professional manner it struck me that he might have done some such job before. I asked him if this was so.

"Yes," he admitted. "I worked in a certain ducal mansion for the past two years, but they must have been afraid that I might sell my story to the Press as they fired me this season. I could have sold it, too. Not that I had much to sell, but I was offered cash."

With this sidelight on the hazards of guiding in stately homes, he took us round efficiently. It is one of those houses, rare in Scotland, which belongs to a family who adhered to the Roman Catholic faith at the Reformation. Due to this and the prolonged lives of the last earl and his sister it has survived with a distinctly 'pickled in aspic' atmosphere, as if time had stood still somewhere around the middle of the eighteenth century. If only for this reason, it is well worth a visit.

Outside Traquair we saw a notice: "To the Blanket Preaching". This was enough to set us in the direction indicated, filled with curiosity, but with no clear idea of what we were going to find at the other end. The road wound over the hills and finally led us down to the Yarrow Water. It soon transpired that we had been fortunate enough to chance on the one Sunday in the year when an open-air service is held in the ruins of the old chapel above St. Mary's Loch. There were many cars parked beside the loch and the Moffat pipe band was in attendance. It was clearly an occasion.

We climbed the hill to the old ruins, of which not much more than the surrounding wall and the graveyard remain. The open-air service was in progress. We stayed to the end and enquired as to the origins and reasons for it. Astonishingly enough, no one, even the minister, seemed quite certain as to the origins of it, although he informed us that it was stipulated in his charge that he should hold it once a year. It appears that it is a memorial to the Covenanters who roamed the hills in the days of persecution. The name 'blanket preaching' refers to the plaid, which used to be held over the preacher to protect him from the weather. At one time such services were common.

Legend has it that the minister hereabouts was a turncoat and was betraying the Covenanters hiding in the hills to the dragoons. He was said to have been shot and buried in an unhallowed grave outside St. Mary's churchyard. A cairn is said to mark the spot, but the likelihood is that this is of much older origin. Much of the Covenanters' 'history' of 'persecution' has to be treated with caution. Although the Covenanters began simply as an anti-papacy religious party at the time of James VI, and took their name from various Covenants signed (notably one in 1581), the move of the Stuarts to England brought changes. Charles I's attempts to impose episcopal rule on Scotland provoked a violent anti-episcopal reaction which soon developed into anti-Royalism. Most of them took the side of Parliament in the Civil War and when Charles II returned to power in 1662, he declared them illegal. Ministers who would not accept the thirty-nine Articles were evicted, and thereafter they held services in the fields. Excellent propagandists, they managed to present their opponents in the worst possible light and, like all religious zealots, had a good deal of success in encouraging their flock to court martyrdom. It is interesting that the name Whig derives from the Coven-anters, 'whig' being the Scots for whey, because of the "sour milk faces of the south-west lowlands".

St. Mary's Loch and the *Dowie dens o' Yarrow* are inevitably as closely connected with James Hogg, the 'Ettrick Shepherd', as the Eildons and Abbotsford with Scott. Hogg is another of those surprising figures of peasant origin and literary genius, such as Burns and Leyden, whom the Scots produced at the turn of the seventeenth and eighteenth centuries. Though little read today Hogg deserves attention. His work was uneven, but surprisingly varied. Of its kind, his *Larriston of Liddesdale*, already quoted, is as fine as anything written, supremely right in its place. His *Confessions of a Justified Sinner*, which has been reprinted, is a prose work, far ahead of its time as a study in supernatural terror. For genuine emotional appeal his poem to his dog Hector is also outstanding. I include just two verses:

> Come my auld, towzy, trusty friend,
> What gars ye look sae dung wi' wae?
> D'ye think my favour's at an end,
> Because thy head is turning grey?

> When my last bannock's on the hearth,
> Of that thou sanna want thy share;
> While I hae house or hauld on earth,
> My Hector shall hae shelter there.

Yet the remarkable thing is that Hogg was unable to read or write until he was twenty. He taught himself by forming large letters on the rocks while shepherding. Born in 1770, a shepherd's son, he was fortunate to be employed in 1790 by a Mr. William Laidlaw, who appears to have been a most under-standing employer, allowing him the run of his library. Hogg's first major work was published in 1801 and in 1802 he met

Scott, who was a source of continual encouragement to him. The story of the shepherd's first visit to Scott's home in Edinburgh is delightful:

When Hogg entered the drawing-room, Mrs Scott, being at the time in delicate state of health, was reclining on a sofa. The Shepherd, after being presented and making his best bow, forthwith took possession of another sofa placed opposite to hers, and stretched himself thereupon at his full length; for, as he said afterwards, "I thought I could never do wrong to copy the lady of the house."

His most profitable early work was *The Shepherd's Guide, being a practical treatise on the Diseases of Sheep*, but although he made enough from this to buy a sheep farm, unfortunately he proved such an incompetent sheep farmer that he went bankrupt. He then took up freelance literary work in Edinburgh and his reputation was finally made with a lengthy poem *The Queen's Wake*, published in 1813. Established after this by the Duke of Buccleuch on a farm in Yarrow at a nominal rent he continued to write, to support his farming. Unfortunately, he seemed to have a knack of choosing incipient bankrupts as his publishers. Then in 1820 he married well and found himself possessed of a farm and land of his own. Like Scott, though on a minor scale, he held open house and was famed for his hospitality, being noted as possessor of "the best trout in Yarrow, the finest lambs on its braes, the finest grouse on its hills, and as good as a *'sma' still* besides". He died in 1835.

A good-looking medium-sized man, Hogg has been accused of many faults, particularly vanity, rudeness and uncouthness. Even if true, which is questionable, it would not have been surprising considering his upbringing and background. The accounts of his famous parties with Christopher North and many literary figures in the renowned inn at the head of St. Mary's Loch run by the colourful landlady Tibbie Shiel, rather conflict with such criticisms. A man who could shout out when dry from talking, "Bring in the loch, Tibbie", as he did on one occasion, must have had the spark of good fellowship as well as genius. He may have been a complex character, but what else could be expected?

Today James Hogg is where he belongs. Though buried in Ettrick churchyard, the poet's statue in bronze, seated with his dog Hector by his side (see pl. 22), stands at the head of St. Mary's Loch, outside 'Tibbie Shiel's Inn', looking towards the famous Grey Mare's Tail, the waterfall he knew so well during his lifetime.

CHAPTER 8

St. Mary's Loch to Dumfries

As on the banks o' wandering Nith
Ae smiling morn I strayed
And traced its bonnie howes and haughs,
Where linties sang and lambkins played

The worm that gnawed my bonnie trees
That reptile wears a Ducal Crown.

ROBERT BURNS, 1759–1796

THE HILLS around St. Mary's Loch and the 'bonny vale of
Yarrow' have so often been the subject of literary outpourings
that they are drenched in the aura of romance. Yet even those
who go to view them sceptically, as Wordsworth did and as
many probably do, cannot help in the end being impressed by
them. Even today with the endless procession of motor cars
and the hordes of visitors they remain bluey green and misty,
intangibly remote from it all (see pl. 24). Here the Cymbric
legends of King Arthur and his knights seem suddenly alive
and possible. An arm in 'white samyte' protruding above the
surface of the loch and holding a gleaming sword would be no
particular surprise. It is doubtful, however, whether any of the
passing motorists would give it more than a second glance and
wonder vaguely what was being advertised.

My friend insisted on a swim. The water looked cold, dark
and forbidding, but we found a shallow, sunwarmed spot,
where a burn runs into it. In the background a yacht race was
taking place. The blue nylon sails of the dinghies bobbed and

dipped, scudding before the wind down to the boathouse. Against the greeny blue of the hills and the dark surface of the loch they made an attractive picture.

We drove on past the bronze statue of James Hogg and Tibbie Shiel's Inn, past the loch of the Lowes, where the hills suddenly close in impressively. We stopped opposite the 'Grey Mare's Tail'. The Rev. Alexander Brown, minister of Moffat in 1791, writing in the *Statistical Account*, noted:

The water issuing from Lochskeen forms a considerable rivulet; and after running near three quarters of a mile, falls from one precipice to another, from a great height, dashing and foaming, and thundering between two high, steep and rocky hills; forming the cascade known by the name of the Grey Mare's Tail. It is seen to the greatest advantage after a heavy rain; when it appears like one unbroken sheet of water from top to bottom.

On the subject of Loch Skeen, he wrote: "The only lake in the parish, it is 1100 yards in length, of unequal breadth. Where broadest about 400 yards. The depth is not known. There is a small island in it, where the eagles bring out their young in great safety."

Since it would be an easy flight over to Innerleithen across the Tweedsmuir hills it is clear that at that time eagles must have been common visitors there. Though much rarer today, their presence becomes more readily understandable on realising that they bred here in the past. Unfortunately we were not able to spare the time to climb up to Loch Skeen. Notices warned that the climb, though deceptively easy-looking, was dangerous. Even the short scramble we took to view the waterfall properly proved extremely slippery on the short grass. The waterfall itself is impressive, but it is easy to understand that the path beside it could be treacherous.

We returned to the car, where we found sheep all round us in the car park. It was obvious that they were accustomed to being fed by visitors. We watched them being offered sandwiches and other unsheeply fare. They appeared to have acquired a taste for such delicacies, but we wondered how many died as a result each year. It is remarkable that in spite of notices requesting them not to feed animals people will still persist in giving them food which is liable to kill them. It is a mistaken kindness and a part of the sentimental woolly thinking of so many townspeople who visit the country today.

We followed the Moffat Water between the impressive hills until eventually we saw the township nestling in a hollow amid the hills. The grey slate roofs glinting in the sunlight gave a welcome promise of relief from the sternness of the country through which we had passed. It was certainly a relief to find ourselves shortly afterwards 'taking tea' in unmistakeably Scots surroundings, heavy mahogany sideboard, spotlessly aproned waitress, oatcakes and jelly, fresh scones and butter, boiled eggs and iced cakes.

Writing in the *Statistical Account* of 1834 the Rev. Alexander Johnstone noted on Moffat:

The habits of the people are particularly decent and cleanly and their language is among the best samples of English to be found in any Scottish village. The grey plaid thrown round the body or across one shoulder and under the opposite arm is still common . . . There is hardly any smuggling or poaching and low and gross acts of immorality are seldom heard of in Moffat.

Writing over forty years earlier in 1791 in the previous *Statistical Account*, the Rev. Alexander Brown does not include such a revealing sidelight, but describes Moffat as follows:

The principal street is wide and spacious . . . There are two mineral springs in the parish: both well known and justly celebrated for their medicinal virtues. The first has long ago been distinguished by the name of Moffat Well and is a strong sulphureous water about a mile and a half from the village . . .

This well was discovered more than 150 years ago; and has ever since been much resorted to from all parts of the kingdom.

The "principal street" is still "wide and spacious" even though now filled with motor cars parked at both sides and two deep in the centre. In a prominent position in the very centre of it stands a handsome life-sized statue of a copper ram on a boulder base, indicating that this is now a sheep centre. Closer examination shows that this statue was presented to the town in 1875, by which time the transition from a prominent spa for invalids 'taking the waters' was almost complete. Yet such changes rarely take effect overnight. Moffat still has a strong look of a Scots Tunbridge Wells or Cheltenham.

We went in search of 'Moffat Well'. Eventually, after one or two false casts and several times being assured "There's nothing there now", we arrived at the end of a road called Moffat Well Head. Apart from a small cottage, which looked something like an old toll house, and a gate into a field, there did indeed seem to be nothing to see. While my friend turned the car, with some difficulty in the restricted space, I knocked on the door of the cottage. Somehow I gained the impression that I was not the first to enquire for the well as my reception was not at first encouraging. Fortunately my attention was caught by a blue-grey kitten.

"Unusual colouring that kitten has," I commented.

"That's not a kitten, it's a full-grown cat," was the reply.

"Surely not," I protested. "It can't be."

It transpired that Mrs. Baker, whose address actually was 'The Old Well', bred these miniature cats and after a conversation on cats and dogs I brought the subject back to the well. This time I was told we were welcome to look at it, but it was again reiterated that there was nothing to see. According to the Rev. Brown, however, in 1791 there was "a long room and stables and other conveniences, upon the spot, for the use of the company when they are drinking the waters".

We walked down to the shed pointed out to us, above a small rocky glen, through which a burn in spate thundered with considerable noise. We slid back the entrance door of this wooden shed, which was about the size of a two-car garage, and found ourselves unexpectedly in a perfect Georgian Pump Room such as many spas around the country must have had at one time. Derelict this one might be, but the essentials were there. The mahogany bench round the walls, the mahogany front to the marble bar counter, even the mahogany till, now empty, in front of the well itself, a narrow fissure in the rock against which the shed was set, were all as they had been. This was undoubtedly the Rev. Brown's "long room".

We went round the counter to examine the well. The Rev. Brown wrote:

Most wonderful cures have been effected by it. For many years past it has been generally used, and with equal success, for creating appetite, and promoting digestion; for bilious and other complaints of the stomach and bowels; for the gravel and the rheumatism . . . It sparkles in the glass like champaign and is so remarkably volatile, that it cannot be drunk in perfection, unless at the fountain.

The cleft in the moss-covered rocks contained a dark pool of nauseous smelling liquid which both looked and smelt as if diesel oil had been poured into it. Unbiased descriptions of the taste of the original waters varied from: "stale eggs whipped up in lucifer matches" to "bilge water, or the scourings of a foul gun". It may be therefore that the well is still as beneficial as ever, but neither my companion nor I felt inclined to try it. If that is how it always was the original discoverer of it in 1633, Miss Rachel Whiteford, daughter of Bishop Whiteford, was a remarkably brave woman.

Standing by the marble counter it was not difficult to picture the scene in the eighteenth century with the elderly vale-tudinarians of both sexes arriving each day to drink their pre-scribed doses of these evil-tasting waters; the returned nabob from India with parchmenty face and white hair, the gouty laird and the retired dragoon, purple-complexioned with grog noses, and the elderly ladies accompanied by their uncomplaining daughters or attendant companions. One can readily see them all gathering there, shuddering slightly as they quickly downed their daily glassful, and lingering to discuss the weather and their ailments with unfailing pleasure.

Leaving the well, we took a walk round the field behind it. There we encountered two elderly ladies taking a stroll from whom we had earlier enquired the way. Although they had assured us that there was nothing to see it now occurred to me that they might know when the well was last in use. I enquired.

"When I was a little girl before the first world war," one replied at once, "I remember seeing horse charabancs and carriages driving up here regularly. In those days there used to be a shop sold sweeties and lemonade as well."

The field we were standing in was probably that mentioned by the Rev. Brown:

As an additional inducement to the invalid to repair to Moffat, a considerable number of goats are kept in the neighbourhood of the well. The pasture is thought to be excellent and the milk of the best kind. It is sent to the village now every morning and every evening.

We drove back into Moffat down what the Rev. Brown described as "an excellent carriage road". With its Georgian overtones, there is no denying that this is an attractive small town. To appreciate its chief interests today it is perhaps best seen at the annual Show. There is nothing valetudinarian about this. There is a noticeable interest in horses with a number of classes including jumping. There is also wrestling, but prominent are the sheepdog trials and above all there are sheep.

Leaving Moffat we crossed the river Annan. It was under a bridge over the Annan close to Moffat that an unfortunate female visitor in 1935 suddenly saw, to her horror, a human hand protruding from a bundle. In subsequent searches over the surrounding moors the police discovered the remains of two women. With remarkable skill these were identified and the hysterical murderer Dr. Buck Ruxton from Lancaster was at once uncovered.

It was a sordid, stupid story of an unbalanced love-hate relationship between the Eurasian doctor, whose real name was Hakim, and his Scots mistress. They were constantly quarrelling and it appears that one day he went too far and strangled her in a fit of rage. The unfortunate girl who worked in the house must either have witnessed the scene or been involved in it for she was also murdered. In frantic efforts to avoid detection, he then dissected the bodies, removing all identifying marks, and distributed the pieces over the barren moors between Moffat and Beattock. Apart from the ghoulish method of disposal of the bodies, which ensured his place in Madame Tussaud's Chamber of Horrors, the case was only remarkable for the skill of the forensic surgeons involved.

We drove on to the Devil's Beef Tub, once known as the Marquis of Annandale's Beef Tub, where the Border reivers at one time kept their stolen cattle and sheep safely penned. It is a vast hollow in the hills, a tremendous yawning natural basin with almost perpendicular sides. The Jacobite innkeeper of the nearby Crook Inn was captured at Culloden and on his way to trial at Carlisle escaped from his guards by boldly wrapping his plaid round himself and diving head first over the edge. Looking down one feels that he earned his successful escape.

At the principal vantage point, a small Celtic cross has been erected (see pl. 25). On the base is this inscription:

To the memory of
John Hunter
Covenanter
Shot in the hills opposite
In the year 1675
By Douglas's Dragoons
Erected 1955

My friend examined this in silence for some minutes after reading the inscription carefully.

"There's no sign as to who erected this," he said finally. "I suppose it's another way of saying 'English Go Home'."

Nor is there any sign as to who, or what society in 1931 erected a circular stone monument by the roadside a little further on to the memory of Guard McGeorge and driver Goodfellow of the mail coach, who perished in a blizzard in 1831 while trying to carry the mail through on foot after the coach had stuck. It seems that McGeorge was a dour and obstinate ex-soldier who had previously been reprimanded by the company for some alleged inattention to duty and was determined to allow no repetition. When the coach stuck fast he announced his determination to go on with the mail. Goodfellow apparently lived up to his name and accompanied him. Next day the mail bags were found by the roadside further on, but there was no trace of the men. Their bodies were not found for nearly a week, buried in snow some distance from the road.

It is not far beyond here close to some newly afforested ground that the Tweed has its source. There is such a tremendous watershed in these hills that it is soon gurgling and chuckling by the roadside in quite sizeable proportion on the earliest stages of its ninety-seven miles to the sea. This is the limit of Colonel Ryan's protectorate, but as each tributary is also within his province it is easy to see how wide his bounds extend.

We soon passed the church at Tweedsmuir where John Hunter the Covenanter lies buried and beyond that the Crook Inn where the Jacobite landlord hid himself after his successful escape from his guards by rolling down the Devil's Beef Tub. From here we turned towards Skirling. The name Carmichael, notable in the Borders for the Redeswire affray and many another incident, was long associated with Skirling. In the eighteenth century the Carmichaels were listed as the principal landowners. There are still Carmichaels in Skirling today.

We called by appointment to see the house and garden created by Lord Carmichael on his retirement as Governor of Bengal prior to his death in 1926. I had been given the impression that wrought iron ran riot here to the extent of a garden full of wrought-iron flowers. Certainly the house at the edge of the village green is noticeable for the wrought-iron railings decorated with fanciful wrought-iron figures, from dragons to top-hatted manikins. In front of the house a wrought-iron hound courses eternally after a wrought-iron hare.

It seems that Lord Carmichael, inspired originally by the intricacy of the famous closed Lion Gates at Traquair, encouraged Thomas Haddon, the wrought-iron artist in Edinburgh, to produce work for him of a similar nature. What started as a mild interest appears to have become an overmastering passion. Inside the house it was restricted to decorative covers for the central heating units, an impressive array of bolts on the front door and wrought-iron latches on most of the doors. Outside freer play was given to the artist's and his patron's imaginations, although not perhaps to quite the over-wrought extent I had been led to expect.

Inside the garden gate, with its decorative wrought-iron inlay, is a massive chunk of metal mastiff, teeth bared in his flat skull, a wrought-iron Cerberus standing guard. Further on are more delicate examples of Haddon's art. Stands for rambler roses are topped with wrought-iron flowers. In this way a dozen or so irises, lilies, tulips and, appropriately, red-hot pokers stand out in full bloom against the winter skies. On a wrought-iron window-box holder is a splendid showing of wrought-iron roses. Beside them stands a wrought-iron rabbit and at a nearby french window a wrought-iron pig acts as a foot-scraper (see pll. 26 and 27). Perhaps the most intricate work of all is a magnificent 'devil atop the world' as a wrought-iron weathervane. Pleasant quirk though all this is, it scarcely amounts to a folly in an age when these are mostly concrete and municipal.

24. "Even today, with the endless procession of motor cars and the hordes of visitors, the hills around St. Mary's Loch remain bluey green and misty, intangibly remote from it all" (p. 140)

25. "The Devil's Beef Tub—where the Border reivers kept their stolen cattle and sheep safely penned—a tremendous yawning natural basin." Near Moffat (p. 14

26. "Wrought-iron roses—delicate examples of Thomas Haddon's art." In Lo Carmichael's garden at Skirling (p. 148)

7. "Wrought-iron flowers stand out in full bloom against the winter sky." Also at Skirling

28. "In the main street of Dumfries beside the notably rococo fountain decorate
with cherubs and looking towards the Mid-Steeple" (p. 159)

For a folly belonging to an earlier age we drove through Biggar to Culter. Here we stopped at Culter House, the home of Lord Ferrier, one of the first to be created a life peer. Returning to his native heath after the war, following a successful business career in India, Lord Ferrier placed his administrative and financial talents freely at the disposal of the Church of Scotland. The Scottish Church, of course, has no bishops and it lacked representatives in the House of Lords. When Lord Ferrier became a life peer he was naturally well informed on Church matters in Scotland, but it would be indiscreet because of this to compare him with a bishop. His half-timbered seventeenth-century whitewashed house is most attractive. At the back, out of sight of the road, is the most magnificent avenue of trees a hundred yards across and a mile long, leading apparently absolutely nowhere.

The Rev. William Strachan, writing on Culter in 1791 in the *Statistical Account*, noted: "Part of the ground is so plain that an avenue to a gentleman's seat in this parish, though upwards of a mile in length is perfectly level." It certainly is level. It has been used by the Royal Company of Archers as a site for their annual match and it would be hard to imagine a better one. The trees, magnificent mature specimens, vary from oak, beech and chestnut to elm. At any time of the year they present an impressive spectacle, but perhaps in the autumn as the leaves are turning they are at their best.

"What is its history?" I asked.

"There used to be two cousins named Dickson," Lord Ferrier explained. "Back in the seventeenth century. One of them owned this house and the other owned Hartree house a couple of miles or so away. In those days this was very boggy country and they agreed each to make a mile-long avenue to join up and provide a two-mile ride between their houses. Unfortunately only one cousin completed his avenue. The one at Hartree died before starting his."

Hartree House, much rebuilt in the nineteenth century, is

now a hotel. It is incidentally almost the only hotel in the Borders area which offers grouse shooting to its guests. The proprietor, Major Dunlop, invited us to shoot on his moor at Over Fingland in the Lowther hills on the Duke of Buccleuch's property. Opening the season on the 12th with ten guns he had fifty-three brace in what was generally not a good season. Although hotel shoots are often "akin to war" it was noticeable that most of his guests obviously knew each other well and were experienced shots.

Driving down to the moor we crossed the main Carlisle to Glasgow dual-carriageway road, which was still in process of construction. It is a formidable engineering feat going through wild and hilly country. Gradients were being levelled, rivers bridged and the appearance of the countryside altered. A long fresh scar of newly turned red earth was being rapidly filled with gleaming concrete. The only dual-carriageway through the Borders at present it must, in due course, be followed by others. Roads suitable for stagecoaches simply cannot cope with modern traffic.

It was noticeable that as soon as we crossed the boundary into Lanark the road surfaces turned at once to a red colour. So noticeable was this that we did not need the county boundary sign to tell us when we passed from Lanarkshire on into Dumfriesshire. The darker road surface in front of us told its own story.

The frowning Lowther hills on this county boundary have a dark history. It was here that suicides used to be buried. Dr. John Brown, sacrificing perhaps some degree of accuracy in his desire to make his reader's blood curdle, wrote:

The bodies were brought from great distances all round, and in accordance with the dark superstitions of the time, the un-blest corpse was treated with curious indignity . . . the body was thrust with the clothes it was found in into a rude box, not even shaped like a coffin, and hurried away on some old shuttered cart or sledge with ropes for harness. One can imagine the miserable procession as it slunk, often during the night, through the villages and past the farm steads, everyone turning from it as abhorred. Then arrived at this high and desolate region, the horse was taken out and the weary burden dragged with pain up to its resting place . . . then a shallow hole dug and the long uncouth box pushed in—the cart and harness left to rot as accursed The white human bones may sometimes be seen among the thick short grass; and one that was there more than fifty years ago remembers, with a shudder still, coming—when crossing the hill top—upon a small outstretched hand, as of one crying from the ground; this one little hand, with its thin fingers held up to heaven, as if in agony of supplication or despair. What a sight to see against the spotless sky, or crossing the disk of the waning moon!

The moor where the suicides were buried is the boundary one, where the Buccleuch lands end today as they ended then. It was held then to be boundary land on the boundary of two counties and three estates, therefore belonging to no one in particular. The part he owns is shot by the Duke of Buccleuch himself. Over Fingland moor, the hotel shoot, is more to the south-west of Wanlockhead, the lead-mining village, the highest village in the Borders. Although the moor could no doubt be approached from the spectacular road down the Mennock Pass beyond Wanlockhead, the southern road through Elvanfoot makes an easier approach.

We stretched our legs on the moor and investigated the shoot. The low-lying part is inclined to be boggy, but there seemed to be plenty of birds and good young coveys strong on the wing. The Lowther hills rising steeply towards Wanlockhead, dark and heather-clad, scarred here and there with fissures and faults in the rock, are gloomy and forbidding. With the sun shining, however, it is easy enough to forget their history.

Writing of this part of the country in the *Statistical Account* prior to 1800, the Rev. William Ranken observed:

There are abundance of grouse, partridges and some black game. The last are more rarely to be met than formerly . . .

chiefly owing to the depradations of poachers, who, favoured by a wide range of uninhabited country, load themselves with booty and frequently escape with impunity. A covey, or rather part of a covey of ptarmigans, among common grouse, a few years ago, was discovered upon the hills, which was considered a curiosity.

It was William Douglas of nearby Fingland who, at the turn of the seventeenth century, fell in love with a girl living not far from Dumfries. Her parents disapproved and the match fell through. Both he and the girl married elsewhere, but in the meantime he had written some deathless verse about her. Part ran:

> She's backit like the peacock;
> She's breastit like the swan,
> She's jimp about the middle;
> Her waist ye well micht span;
> And she has a rollin' eye;
> And for bonnie Annie Laurie,
> I'd lay me doun and die.

These and other verses were the ones Lady John Scott adapted and set to music to produce the famous *Annie Laurie*. Though perhaps her verses may be more presentable I feel one gets a clearer picture of the lady from William Douglas's version. 'Jimp about the middle' with 'a rolling eye' sounds more human, if a lot more flighty, than the swan-necked creature portrayed by Lady John Scott, of whom I have always been a trifle suspicious. He was probably well rid of her, though his protestations of eternal affection seem somewhat weak in view of the fact that he was the first to marry another.

The verses by Burns at the head of this chapter relate to the despoliation of Nithsdale by 'Old Q', the last Duke of Queensberry, to finance his spendthrift illegitimate daughter the Marchioness of Hertford and also to spite the Buccleuchs whom he knew must succeed him. He cut down vast areas of timber and laid bare whole forests systematically round Drumlanrig. Drumlanrig mansion itself he entirely neglected.

Although not open to the public today, since it is still lived in by the Duke of Buccleuch, as an alternative home to Bowhill, Drumlanrig merits more than a passing mention. Built round a quadrangle in the ten years between 1679 and 1689 for the 1st Duke of Queensberry, the direct descendant of the Douglases, it is a massive pile. It has been likened to Heriot's Hospital in Edinburgh, although Drumlanrig is decidedly over-balustraded in comparison. It is certainly most beautifully placed above the Nith Valley and in a natural basin in the hills.

The story behind its building is even more remarkable than the end product. The first Duke, something of a hypochondriac, was in a petulant mood when he finally moved into his vast new mansion. One can imagine the scene. Everything richly laid out, new sumptuous tapestries, rich furnishings, pictures and ornaments, but nothing somehow quite to the Duke's taste. The local doctor was a fool. There was a draught where-ever one moved. The chimneys smoked abominably. It was quite impossible to be comfortable. After only one sleepless night in his new house the Duke ordered his bags to be packed and left it again for ever. Only the bills remained to be paid and it seems they were large enough to affect even the Duke's vast fortune, for in a fit of pique he scrawled across the accounts: "The De'eil pike out his een who looks herein." Clearly he regarded Drumlanrig as one of his worst investments, but with truly ducal pride and philosophy shrugged his losses aside and never visited the place again.

In 1770 Pennant visited Drumlanrig and wrote:

In my walk about the park, see the white breed of wild cattle, derived from the native race of the country, and still retain the primeval savageness and ferocity of their ancestors; were more shy than any deer; ran away on the appearance of any of the human species; and even set off at full gallop on the least noise, so that I was under the necessity of going very softly under the shelter of trees or bushes to get a near view of them. During summer they keep apart from all other cattle; but in severe weather hunger will compel them to visit the out-houses in search of food. The keepers are obliged to shoot them if any are wanted; if the beast is not killed on the spot, it runs at the person who gave the wound, and who is forced, in order to save his life, to fly for safety to the intervention of some tree. These cattle are of the middle size, have very long legs . . . the orbits of the eyes and the tips of the noses are black . . .

It seems that 'Old Q' disposed of this herd at some time before his death in 1810, probably not so very long after Pennant's visit.

We drove down the attractive valley of the Nith towards Dunscore. The Rev. Joseph Kirkpatrick, writing in the *Statistical Account* in 1792, recorded:

The black cattle in general are of the Galloway breed; but Mr. Robert Burns, a gentleman well known by his poetical productions, who rents a farm in this parish, is of the opinion that the west-country cows give a larger production of milk.

These "west-country" cows were, of course, Ayrshires, today recognised as one of the leading milking breeds, so that Burns seems to have been a sound enough judge, even if, like Hogg his farming was conducted at a loss.

On our way to Dunscore we stopped at the tower of Lag, recently taken over by the National Trust for Scotland. Little remains of what was once a high and narrow peel tower belonging to the notorious Sir Robert Grierson of Lag, who with General Dalyell of the Binns and John Graham of Claverhouse, Viscount Dundee, was amongst the most infamous of persecutors of the Covenanters. Sir Robert Grierson's name has been used as a by-word to frighten young children in Dumfriesshire and Galloway ever since his death, so much so that I was assured that young girls even today refuse to go past this tower alone at night. It is only fair to remember, of course, that young girls always like an excuse for a companion.

There are many legends concerning this man Grierson of Lag, who died aged over eighty in the year 1733. There are tombstones with "Shot to death by Grier of Lag". It is said he hanged Covenanters without trial. One of his favourite customs was supposedly to sit at the window of his tower in Lag and watch Covenanters being rolled down Halliday Hill opposite in spiked barrels. He ordered the death of two young girls by drowning at stakes in the Solway unless they recanted, and both were drowned. He was a false coiner. He swore, blasphemed, drank and debauched all his life until in the end just retribution caught up with him.

His death was sensational. It seems that for weeks beforehand he had to employ relays of servants to fetch buckets of water from the Nith to pour over his gouty feet. When they did so the water was seen to steam and sizzle. Finally, after a week's debauch, he died, but he was so corpulent that the wall of the house where he was staying in Dumfries had to be broken down to get his coffin out to the hearse. Once there, though the horses sweated and steamed, they seemed unable to move it. Finally a close friend harnessed a team of thoroughbreds, which at once bolted at a wild and uncontrollable gallop straight to the gate of Dunscore Church, where they halted in a lather of foam and fell dead on the spot. Throughout these entire proceedings it seems a raven, bird of ill omen, had maintained its perch on the presumably wildly rocking coffin.

Hardly one word of all this was true. The Covenanters appear to have had a quite remarkable ability to distort the facts and this Jacobite laird seems to have been a much maligned man. He seems to have had a coarseness and directness of speech common to his age and to have been far from teetotal, but apart from that and having backed the wrong side by staying loyal to the Stuarts, there is little that can really be held against him. His evil reputation is an example of how far the rabid zealotry of the Whig Covenanters could be carried in twisting the truth. A more obvious example concerns another Tory laird nearby, Laurie of Maxwellton, the famous Annie's father. Supposedly noted for his bloody persecutions also, it stated that on one occasion a glass of claret he was drinking turned to blood.

The most heroic story concerning the Jacobites of Niths-dale is undoubtedly Lady Nithsdale's courageous last-minute rescue of her husband, the Earl of Nithsdale, from the Tower of London, the day before he was due to be executed for his part in the rebellion of 1715. Astonishingly, she managed to smuggle him out dressed as her pregnant female companion and thereafter arranged his escape to France. As an example of feminine determination to save her man, this exceeds even Dorothy Forster's rescue of her brother from Newgate prison at about the same time.

It is noticeable throughout the *Statistical Account*, but par-ticularly in Dumfriesshire, that the clergymen are at pains to stress the religious toleration of their parishes, by way of contrast to the days of the Covenanters, only a century earlier. Referring to the religious attitudes of the various groups which had seceded from the established church, one minister wrote: "If they are disappointed of their own pastor, most of them do not scruple to hear the nearest established minister." A story told me by a minister's daughter from these parts, however, summed it all up for me. It seems that a couple who had been absent from the church for nearly a year unexpectedly returned to the fold. At the church door after the service he greeted them:

"I'm glad to see you back."

"Weel, minister, ye ken it's like this. First we tried the Free Kirk, then we tried the Wee Frees and then we tried the Baptists and noo we've given up religion a'tegither and we've come back tae you."

We drove on beyond Dunscore, where the countryside for a

space looks rather, as my companion remarked, as if it had come out in a crop of boils. The land is known locally as "a' stanes an' gravel". The mounds are due to generations of removing stones from the fields. Apart from this, the small whitewashed farmhouses with their crow-stepped gables are typical of the pleasant pastoral Dumfriesshire countryside, which merges with the green hills of Galloway in the west. It was in such a farmhouse "16 miles from a baker" at Craigenputtock that Thomas Carlyle lived with his wife in the early years of their marriage.

We drove towards the Galloway hills to see by appointment a collection of some outstanding works by Epstein, Henry Moore and other sculptors of note. Their owner has conceived the brilliant idea of placing them on natural sites around the landscape on his estate so that a Henry Moore reclines on a knoll above the heather and 'The Visitation' by Epstein stands in a ring of trees on a hillside (see pll. 29, 30, 31). In front of the house itself is a splendid bronze head of a boy by Renoir and a most attractive dog by Epstein.

The headkeeper, who showed us round, was noticeably less than enthusiastic about the sightseers who from time to time park beside the public road nearby and trespass on the moor itself. Noting a number of pheasant poults just ready to go into covert I understood how he felt about this. It must be something of a headache from the game preserver's viewpoint as well as for the owner.

Hearing a rustling underfoot I looked round just in time to see a distinctive v-back adder slithering away through the undergrowth.

"Do you get many snakes here?" I asked.

"Oh, aye, quite a few," was the reply.

I wondered how many sightseers would bother to make the journey if they knew of the existence of such a hazard. At the same time this must be unique in being the only shoot in the country where one might find oneself standing between an

Epstein and a Henry Moore waiting for the high birds to come over. It is a pleasant concatenation of tastes.

Turning towards Dumfries we approached it first by way of Maxwelltown, which has no connection with Annie Laurie, but is now merely a suburb of Dumfries. On the west side of the Nith it used to be the haunt of all the undesirables of the town in the sixteenth century. Today it includes one of the items most worth seeing in Dumfries, namely the museum. Housed in a tower, once a windmill, this contains what is claimed to be the oldest camera obscura in the country, dating from 1836.

No one visiting Dumfries should miss this splendid museum. It includes the most happily haphazard collection of *memorabilia* about Dumfries and its environs it would be possible to imagine. Neatly printed notices on the walls and above the exhibits make fascinating and sometimes confusing reading. Legend, lore and fact are so inextricably intermixed it is almost impossible to separate one from the other, but one soon appreciates that Dumfries, Border town though it may be, is also the gateway to the west where the belief in fairies, witches and wizards is a long time dying. Reading these notices one learns such exotic points as "Sodomites and their horses were hung from a special hill". Further on is a note to the effect that in 1786 a little man in a green hat was hatched from an egg.

There are a number of bridges over the Nith and a notable cauld. According to the Rev. Morton in the *Statistical Account* of 1845:

The Nith and all its branches are poached without interruption during the whole of the close season, and to such an extent that in the general opinion for every salmon taken in the open or legal season, more than thirty are destroyed in the close period—a practice which ruins the health, destroys the industry, corrupts the morals and familiarising the mind to habitual and open violations of the law, seldom fails to terminate in atrocious and daring deeds of wickedness. While, by the toleration of such irregular deeds thousands of parent fishes are destroyed in the breeding season . . .

He went on to attribute much of this to the cauld across the water at Dumfries and ended: "Fishings which were formerly of great value are at present worth little or nothing."

Surprisingly enough, this state of affairs continued until the formation of a Fishing Improvements Association in 1934. Even then it was not until after the 1939–45 war that matters began to be taken seriously in hand. Burgh nettings below the cauld were strictly checked and the various caulds across the river throughout its length were constructed to allow the salmon easy passage. Since then, over each five-year period, there has been an outstanding increase in the numbers of fish caught, as much as five times as many salmon, ten times as many grilse and seven times as many sea trout. Such figures speak for themselves.

Standing in the Main Street of Dumfries beside the notably rococo fountain decorated with cherubs (see pl. 28) and looking towards the old town house known as the Mid-steeple, I was reminded that this was once a stronghold of the Maxwells. Traditionally they hated the Johnstons and Jardines, whose rival stronghold once was the town of Lockerbie. By the end of the nineteenth century, though the various families were freely intermixed in Dumfries such feuds were not forgotten. An English traveller stranded there unable to find lodgings for the night was said to have cried out in despair:

"Is there not a Christian in Dumfries who will give a body a bed for the night?"

A window opened and a Maxwell head was briefly poked out before the window slammed shut again:

"There are nae Christians left in Dumfries. Only Johnstons and Jardines."

In spite of this story Dumfries calls its Common Riding Week 'Guid Nychburris Week', from an old custom whereby feuding citizens could be compelled by a magistrate to take an oath to keep 'Gude Nychborhude'. The Marches are ridden and the Cornet and his Lass take part in local ceremonies. These include a historical pageant.

No tour of Dumfries is complete without a visit to the house where Burns lived, or better still, if you are a Burns fan, to his favourite tavern, the Globe Inn (see pl. 23). This is a lively inn where Burns might still feel at home, and where correspondingly the prim and censorious will feel ill at ease, especially in the evenings when a sing-song is at its height. In view of the fact that Dumfries and Bonnie Prince Charlie were not in accord, indeed he 'fined' the town for assaulting his baggage train, it is not surprising that the inn he stayed at was for many years known as the Commercial. It is now called the Kings Arms and the panelled room where Prince Charlie is reputed to have slept is shown with pride.

Anyone who suffers from difficulty in finding the right road out of Dumfries, owing to the totally inadequate signposting, will realise that this has probably not altered since the Rev. William Burnside noted in 1794:

About the beginning of the present century a gentleman from England purchased a quantity of tobacco here and paid down the money for it, but went away without directing whither it should be sent Every enquiry after him proved fruitless In consequence of this the town at length obtained leave from the court of Exchequer to dispose of this tobacco, and apply the price to the purpose of making a road through Lockermoss towards Annan . . . The advantages arising from the improved state of the roads within these 20 or 30 years have been nowhere more sensibly felt than in this parish and neighbourhood.

CHAPTER 9

Dumfries to Spadeadam

O were there war between the lands,
As well I wot that there is nane,
I would slight Carlisle castell high,
Though it were builded of marble stane.

I would set that castell in a low,
And sloken it with English blood!
There's never a man in Cumberland
Should ken where Carlisle castell stood.

'KINMONT WILLIE': TRADITIONAL

WE DROVE from Dumfries towards the Solway, after eventually finding the right road, which led us down beside the estuary of the Nith. It is a pleasant drive past Glencaple, beloved of wildfowlers, with cows grazing on the seaweed and wrack by the tidal foreshore and on the wild grassy flats. The hills of Cumberland, blue and hazy in the distance, are visible across the wide expanse of the Solway Firth.

Our destination was Caerlaverock Castle, which is an unusual ruin. Built in the thirteenth century on a triangular rock in the centre of a marsh it was, of necessity, itself triangular in shape. It belonged to the Maxwell family and suffered the usual chequered fate of the Border castles, being alternatively besieged, sacked and then rebuilt. In the seventeenth century, when the accession of James VI to the throne of England brought peace to the Borders, Robert Maxwell, 1st Earl of Nithsdale, built what was in effect a splendid house in the

Renaissance style inside the castle walls. Unfortunately it was besieged yet again in 1640 when Charles I's supporters under Lord Nithsdale eventually surrendered it to the Covenanters. It was then partially destroyed and has remained a ruin ever since.

The red stone castle was undergoing repairs at the time of our visit. Exploring it was a hazardous proceeding as a result, with only plank bridges across gaping holes. The outside is massive enough at first sight and the unusual shape is obvious. Walking round, or through it, one is unexpectedly confronted with the small, but beautifully proportioned façade of a house, actually tucked away inside the castle itself. In the same attractive stone as the outer walls, each doorway and window has a triangular or semi-circular shaped crest elaborately carved above it. The total effect, especially when the sun is shining on it, is charming.

From Caerlaverock we drove alongside the foreshore for a short distance before striking inland once more towards Torthorwald. On the way we passed Rockhall, another property once owned by Sir Robert Grierson of Lag, where he was charged with having engaged in false coining and where he supposedly hanged Covenanters from a hook in the cellar. Neither story had any foundation in fact.

The Rev. James McMillan in the first *Statistical Account* wrote: "Torthorwald is supposed to signify the Tower of Thor in the Wood." He ascribed it to Saxon origin, but it might be more readily attributed to the Danes, who settled on this coastline fairly extensively. His successor in 1833 noted:

The old castle of Torthorwald is situated near the Church and manse and village of Torthorwald and a great part of the walls are still standing. No decay or dilapidation has taken place since the last Statistical Account; indeed it may stand as it is for many years as the mortar with which it is cemented is as firm as the solid stone.

This was a sound guess, for the remains of the old peel tower are still standing much as he described them. The thick walls are riven with fissures, but the stone is firmly held by the ancient mortar in a solid mass like iron, otherwise it would long ago have been quarried for the stones. With sheep grazing round it and with ivy-clad walls it presents a pleasant peaceful picture like so many of these towers today although no doubt it has known scenes of battle and bloodshed in the past.

It is a short drive to Lochmaben, a small trig town, on the outskirts of which is the loch from which it acquires its name. According to the Rev. Andrew Jaffray in 1794:

The Castle Loch is a large and beautiful sheet of water, lying south of the town, in length a mile and a half, and in mean breadth a mile, abounding in a variety of fish. It is affirmed by fishermen that there are 15 or 16 different kinds fit for the table, among which is one that from every information that can be obtained, is peculiar to that loch and is to be found nowhere else in Britain. It is called the Vendise, or Vendace . . . it is generally about the size of a small herring, which it resembles much in external appearance and in its anatomy; it has the taste and flavour of a fresh herring, not quite so strong, but more delicate, and is reckoned the most delicious fish that swims. They lie in the deepest part of the loch and are caught with a net. The pike which is the tyrant of the lake destroys many of them . . . They have the mark of a heart in the crown of the head.

He went on to note salmon at "3d. a pound".

We drove round the Castle Loch to the ruins on the far side of it from which it takes its name. These consist merely of some grassy mounds and a few fragments of wall; however, I discovered here that the loch and 370 acres surrounding it have been made a nature preserve. Apart from the variety of fish in the loch, the water, it seems, has peculiar properties, being rich in iron and other chemicals, so that rare grasses and flowers grow round the edges. The place is indeed a naturalist's delight.

In a lengthy explanatory notice attached to a map of the area and signed by the Town Clerk it was made clear that this was not intended as any form of restriction, but rather to give everyone a better chance of enjoying the natural flora and fauna. Unfortunately, there is no keeper to administer the reserve and we soon found that some members of the public had taken advantage of the fact. Litter bins ignored and dead fish left to rot by the shore side, showed that there are always those who cannot be trusted not to spoil the pleasures of others.

The loch today is also used for yachting and the smart blue nylon sails of the dinghies enhanced the scene as they skimmed over the water from the small yacht club on the roadside shore. As the sun was shining warmly my friend insisted on bathing, in spite of the breeze. We passed the rival transistor sets of several picnic parties and one or two fishermen spinning hopefully for perch and others of the "15 or 16 different kinds". Finally we reached a comparatively private corner and entered the water. The bottom was muddy, but it shelved comparatively quickly. Though cold, it was a pleasant break on a hot day, but these are not waters to be recommended for non-swimmers.

We continued on towards Lockerbie, crossing a stretch of the river Annan much given to overflowing—to judge by the remains of recent floods. Closer inspection of the map showed that the Dryfe Water joining the Annan a little north of the road was probably the cause of this frequent flooding. It was this junction of Dryfe and Annan, known as Dryfe Sands, which was the scene of a decisive battle in one of the last great Border feuds.

The Maxwells of Nithsdale and the Johnstones, later Lords of Annandale, had long been rivals. By gathering round him many minor lairds, Lord Maxwell gained a powerful ascendancy in numbers. In 1585 he burned Sir James Johnstone's tower at Lochwood. One Maxwell raider reputedly cried out that they would "give Dame Johnstone light enough to see to set her silken hood". In 1593, aided by the Scotts of Buccleuch, the

& 30. "Their owner has conceived the brilliant idea of placing them on natural es—it is a pleasant concatenation of tastes." Two works by Henry Moore (p. 157)

31. "The Visitation by Epstein stands in a ring of trees on a hillside" (p. 1

Armstrongs and the Grahams, Sir James Johnstone defeated a superior force of Maxwells at Dryfe Sands, Lord Maxwell and several hundred of his supporters were killed. Many of the remainder were slashed about the face, marked for life by what came to be known as 'Lockerbie Licks'.

The sequel to it all was the treacherous murder of Sir James Johnstone in 1608, shot in the back by the young Lord Maxwell in the course of a meeting ostensibly to effect a reconciliation. He fled the country promptly, but on his return some years later he was captured and executed at James VI's orders in spite of highly placed intercessions on his behalf. The best thing to come out of the whole sorry story is the rather touching ballad known as *Lord Maxwell's Goodnight*:

> Adieu, Dumfries, my proper place,
> But and Carlaverock fair,
> Adieu, the castle of the Thrieve,
> And all my buildings there.

Lockerbie is a small traffic-ridden town now being by-passed by the vast engineering project of the dual-carriageway between Carlisle and Glasgow. At the moment the constant throb of heavy traffic is still the daily accompaniment of living for the inhabitants. When the new road is complete its quiet charm may be apparent, but the principal business of the people, which at present seems to be supplying bed and breakfast to the passing travellers, will have largely vanished. Lockerbie may then revert to being simply a sheep centre, but such towns are liable to expand vastly as industry realises the value of a centre close to a fast means of communication and a ready labour source.

From Lockerbie we had the choice of visiting Robert the Bruce's cave, or Carlyle's birthplace in Ecclefechan. One cave, we reasoned, is much like another and neither of us admired Carlyle. Apart from that, birthplaces and babies lack all true qualities of character except to those determined to trace them.

M   165

We decided to go fishing instead. We drove down past Castle Milk to the Annan at Hoddam bridge.

As on the Nith conditions on the Annan seem to have improved greatly. In 1796 in the *Statistical Account*, William Stewart, Esq., of Hillside near Lockerbie, wrote:

It is surprising that even proprietors of fishing upon Annan kill salmon down to November and see them destroyed under their own eyes with leister and spear upon the spawn bed. The destruction of the ewe in lamb, or the hen upon eggs in March, would not more demonstrate the impolicy and depravity of man. It is beyond a doubt that salmon return from the sea to the rivers they were bred in, and the fisher is as sure of them as the shepherd the cast of his flock.

About a century earlier prior to the building of the bridge, the Duke of Queensberry's sister, a particularly eccentric figure, lived at Hoddam Castle. In the Hoddam MS is noted:

The Duke's sister, Lady Margaret Jardine, carried love of money to a pitch scarcely credible. Though married to an opulent baronet she would, for a halfpenny, bear people on her shoulders across the river Annan, which flows near the wall of her spouse's mansion; and when there was a fair, or a field preaching, in the neighbourhood would sit on the banks of the stream the whole day in expectation of customers. She generally wore rags; but, when visiting, carried articles of finery in a napkin, which she would slip on before she entered the house.

In the summer when I first stopped at Hoddam bridge to look at the river I saw an old man in a 'twa-snouter' surveying the water with a keen eye; a water bailiff if ever there was one. I joined him. Below us the grassy bank on one side of the river was lined with picnickers and blaring transistor sets.

"Where do they all come from?" I asked.

"Oh, they're a' English," he said. "They come by the cairt load."

"D'you get much poaching?"

"Och, I found yin, no sae lang back, wi' twentyfower parr in his creel, fishin' wi' a maggot," he said disgustedly. "Whit can ye dae wi' yon sort?"

Although this was not his stretch of water, he recommended it, informing me that permits could be obtained from Hoddam Castle. I made a mental note to book a day's fishing there later in the season but, unfortunately, on the occasion of our second visit in September we were unlucky. The water was running high, but not quite as high as the mark on the bridge which allowed spinning. There were plenty of fish in the river, but they played hopscotch with our lines, ignoring our flies no matter how we changed them. I only saw one small and foolish herling caught, though the stretch of river is a very pleasant one indeed.

Surprisingly, most of the fishermen came from England. One dressed in oilskins, waders and beret turned out to be an Italian confectioner from Manchester who had motor cycled up the night before and was motor cycling back again that night. He was a stout sportsman in every sense of the word.

"Do you think the building of the cauld across the river to take water for the Chapelcross power station has done much damage to the fishing?" I asked the keeper.

"It's mebbe not so bad now they've altered it," he admitted grudgingly. "But it made a terrible difference to start with. The fish couldn't get up at all."

The Rev. Richard Nivison, writing at nearby Middlebie in 1832, noted:

Our fuel is peat and coal; the former of which is obtained in mosses, now nearly exhausted by the work of years; the latter is brought from the coal pits of his Grace the Duke of Buccleuch in the parish of Canonbie, distant about twelve miles and from the thriving town of Annan about seven miles distant whither it is conveyed over the Solway from Cumberland.

One cannot help wondering what the Rev. Nivison would

have to say if he could see the enormous bulk of the nuclear
power station at Chapelcross which with its four vast cooling
towers dominates the scene from as far afield as the Debatable
Land below Canonbie and the Solway shore near Caerlaverock
(see pl. 32). It was inevitable that eventually we would approach close to this nuclear eyesore. Since it was the first
Scottish nuclear power station and since it is such a prominent
landmark, my friend argued that I should include it. To cut
short further discussion on the point he drove us across a
disused airfield to the entrance gates; triple barbed wire strands
beneath floodlit chain fences and an enormous notice outside
the hut manned by police made it clear that this was an ex-
clusive area:

"Entrance by Pass Only; All Cameras Forbidden; Beware
Guard Dogs . . . "—the list of impressive threats and regulations was somewhat startling. Beyond it all the multi-coloured
yellow, blue and red piping wound round each of the vast
square concrete nuclear piles in a manner that would have made
a surrealist artist wild with envy. Slowly the policeman at the
gate approached us:

"What were ye wanting?"

We explained and, encouraged by a glint of humour in his
eye, we enquired how long he had been there.

"Ever since they started work on it in 1955."

"And when did they first get it going?"

"They didn't start generating power until 1959, but mind
they had to put in all the parts 'clean', as they called it, so it was
slow work and I don't mind saying we were sweating a bit when
they were connecting it up, but of course it's dead safe now."

"Well, if you've been here since it was just a couple of sparks,
perhaps you can explain how we get permission to see round
it?" my friend demanded.

Thus it was, after writing for permission, which was readily
granted, that I subsequently had my own personal guided tour
round the place, a somewhat reluctant victim of my friend's

enthusiasm. On this second visit by appointment there was quite a squad of police on duty at the main gate and I had to fill in a form before being issued with a pass. I commented on this apparently excessive zeal for security.

"Well, you see," explained my guide, a diplomatic young man, who knew all the answers, "we produce plutonium for defence purposes, but in the main these are just the normal security precautions any large factory insists on."

We took a lift to the top of the first reactor. From a window I caught a glimpse of a magnificent view across the Solway. Then my guide started to draw diagrams lucidly expounding the workings of the whole thing. Surprisingly enough, it is not too difficult to grasp the basic principles, or the general outline.

In effect any generating station requires a source of heat, a boiler to convert water to steam, turbines driven by the steam and alternators driven by them, generating the electricity. Early in the process of discovering nuclear fission it was found that by using a moderating influence the fission, or chain reaction, could be slowed to produce heat instead of an explosion. The moderator used is graphite. Thus each reactor consists basically of a graphite pile in which are inserted alloy cans of uranium fuel and boron rods which control the level of heat and maintain it at a steady level.

To give some idea of its size and complexity the pile consists of 58,000 bricks of graphite measuring 36 feet across by 27 feet high, or rather larger than four double-decker buses side by side. Inside the pile are 1,800 vertical channels: in 1,696 of these uranium fuel is suspended: in 48 are boron control rods: the entire pile is encased in a cylindrical steel tank 2 inches thick, 37 feet in diameter and 70 feet high and around this is a 6-inch steel plate as a thermal shield and 8 inches of concrete on top of that as a biological shield.

Inside this enormous tank and round the pile, carbon dioxide gas is circulated under great pressure to draw off the heat. This immensely hot gas is then put through what is in effect a vast geyser, which turns water to steam to drive the turbines. The whole thing is difficult to visualise when standing on top of the reactor. All that can be seen are the various heavy circular entry hatches through which any leaking fuel units can be removed as soon as the complex detecting apparatus gives warning. In the control room there is more to see, but it is curiously remote. This, one feels, is the height of automation. The modern power technician clad in a spotless white overall sits at a dais surrounded by a vast instrument panel silently controlling the whole thing by altering the setting of a wheel at the flicker of a needle on one of the many dials in front of him. He might be piloting a *Queen Mary* size submarine or a vast space craft. It is strange to think that in twenty years time it may all seem as out of date as a horse and buggy.

"This is more expensive than producing power by coal, isn't it?" I asked.

"At present," admitted my guide. "But so far these stations have only been built one at a time and each has involved improvements in design. Had they been produced in numbers the cost would have been much lower. As it is they are saving millions of tons of coal and by 1970 it is hoped they will be cheaper than coal."

"As I understand it the pile has to be sealed off after a working life of only twenty years. Is that so?"

"For economic calculations the working life is estimated at twenty years, but in practice it is likely to be thirty or more."

"But in fact you couldn't then move the pile. It would have to stay sealed off for a hundred years. Is that right?"

"We could move it, but it would cost about £10,000 a square foot. In the next few years a more economic method of disposal may be discovered. Meanwhile it is simpler and more economic to seal it off and use the instruments and equipment on another pile."

My guide was both patient and helpful and it seemed unfair to badger him further. I left and rejoined my friend both impressed and depressed. Peel towers and even bing heaps were natural products of their ages. It now seems we are contemplating with equanimity leaving our own larger and dangerously radio-active eyesores behind us. It scarcely seems good enough to assume that the next few years will supply us with answers we do not have already. They may—and then again, they may not.

My friend and I stared at the lines of huge pylons marching southwards.

"This should have been built over there on the Debatable Land," he said. "Or perhaps it's debatable whether it should have been built at all. Where do we go now?"

"We can either go south to Annan or north to Kirconnel, to see where Adam Fleming dealt with the dastardly Bell," I replied.

I then had to explain. In the seventeenth century both Fleming and this man Bell loved a girl named Helen Irving, known far and wide as 'Fair Helen'. It is amazing how much trouble blondes seem to have caused through the ages. In this case Bell, furiously jealous of his rival's success, came upon them together near the church. Levelling his musket at Flem-ing, he pulled the trigger. Unfortunately, Helen, rushing be-tween them, received the bullet and promptly expired in Fleming's arms. Bell, appalled at the result of his action, turned to fly, but was seized by Adam Fleming, who in the words of the ballad "hacked him in pieces sma' ". Thereafter Fleming roamed the world enlisting in the equivalent of the Foreign Legion, but he could never forget his beloved Helen. One day the churchgoers arrived to find the corpse of a travel-stained grey-haired man lying across her grave. Examination revealed that it was the missing Adam Fleming and he was buried beside her, thus, according to the ballad, fulfilling his wish:

> Oh, would I were where Helen lies,
> On fair Kirconnel lea!

We took the Annan road, ignoring the advice of one Richard Hall, who was the arch conspirator in the rescue of a friend of his called Archie of Cawfield under sentence of death in Dumfries gaol. According to the ballad *Archie of Cawfield*:

> Some says, "We'll gang the Annan Road;
>   It is the better road," said they;
> But up bespake then Dicky Ha'
>   The wisest of that company.

> Says, "Annan road's a public road,
>   It's no the road that makes for me;
> But we will through at the Hoddam ford,
>   It is the better road," quo' he.

There is a marked similarity between this ballad and the better-known account of the rescue of Kinmont Willie from Carlisle Castle, or that of yet another reiver, Jock o' the Side, from Newcastle gaol. In each case the prisoner was safely carried off in chains as far as a flooded river:

> Oh, there was horsing, horsing in haste,
>   And cracking of whips out owre the lee;
> Until they cam to Annan Water,
>   And it was flowing like the sea.

There follows in each account the successful fording by the pursued to the bafflement of the pursuers. Inevitably there is a great deal of duplication in Border stories and Border ballads, as well as in Border history, sometimes by accident, sometimes by design and sometimes in fact. Another example of this tendency towards duplication is the story connected with the tower of Spedlins, ancient home of the Jardines, further north beside the Annan. It is said that a Jardine rode off to Edinburgh, forgetting that he had locked a miller named Porteous in his dungeon. Discovering the key in his pocket, he at once rode back, only to find he was too late. The man had starved to death, gnawing his hands to the bone. A similar story with much the same grisly details is told of Haughton Castle in Northumberland.

Annan appears to be flourishing. The advent of any works such as Chapelcross employing over a thousand workers must inevitably be reflected in the increasing prosperity of the nearby towns and Annan is no exception. It is not, however, an outstandingly attractive town. We continued straight on to Gretna Green, which is a highly developed tourist trap. With marriage, not divorce, its object it might be termed the miniature Las Vegas of the North without the gambling or the glitter. No doubt without the gambling or the glitter Las Vegas would look as sordid.

Yet, in its way, it is also almost laughable. There is a sign saying "To the Blacksmith's Shop". A little further on is another sign "To the Original Blacksmith's Shop", further on still is "To the one and only genuine Blacksmith's Shop". Another sign reads "Lover's Leap Motel". As Lamberton and Coldstream were once notorious for runaway marriages from England, so once was Gretna Green, but it is the only one of the three that continues to exploit its notoriety. The poor miserable eloping couples still occasionally sucked into the trap and subjected to the full glare of Press publicity are to be pitied—but even more so are those people unfortunate enough to live there who hate the whole degrading business.

We drove on towards Longtown, past the Solway Moss and the Debatable Land to the north. Longtown was laid out as an estate village by Sir James Graham in the eighteenth century. It still has a faintly planned look about it, though it now has a slightly mouldering air as well. The most remarkable feature we noted here was that the young waitress who served us with tea in the hotel made a practice of curtseying on being asked for anything. This bobbing so intrigued my friend that he bought several packets of cigarettes he did not require to make quite certain that his eyes were not deceiving him.

It is no great distance to Carlisle. Unfortunately, once there it cannot be said that there is a great deal for the visitor to see.

The Cathedral has suffered much at various periods in its history. It has a remarkable mis-shapen Norman arch and a fine east window fifty-eight feet high, but it is probably best visited to enjoy the detail of its many carvings and the magnificent view from the tower. It is from here that one realises that Carlisle is today a busy industrial and railway centre. Indeed, if Newtown St. Boswells is the Crewe of the Borders then Carlisle is the St. Pancras and Euston. Looking at the castle and its surroundings it seems a far cry indeed to the days of Kinmont Willie's rescue in 1596 by the 'Bold Buccleuch', who bearded Lord Scrope, the English Warden of the West March, in his headquarters in Carlisle.

It was when he heard of Kinmont Willie's arrest that Buccleuch made his vow quoted at the head of the chapter. After attacking the castle and forcing his way in through a postern door still to be seen, he effected Kinmont Willie's release, all the time making so much noise with his party that it was taken for a large-scale attack, not a matter of a raid by thirty men. Carrying Kinmont Willie with them in chains, they rode back:

> Buccleuch has turned to Eden Water,
> > Even where it flow'd frae bank to brim,
> And he has plunged in wi' a' his band,
> > And safely swam them through the stream.

> He turned him on the other side,
> > And at Lord Scroope his glove flung he,
> If ye like na my visit to merry England,
> > In fair Scotland come visit me!

Lord Scroope, according to the ballad, was left gibbering:

> He is either himsell a devil frae hell,
> > Or else his mother a witch maun be;
> I wadna have ridden that wan water,
> > For a' the gowd in Christentie.

174

Carlisle still suffers, or benefits, whichever way it is viewed, from an influx of Irish munition workers during the first world war. They caused so many accidents by mixing gun-cotton with alcohol that the government was forced to nationalise all the public houses and the local brewery. Thus in Carlisle and for quite an area around all the inns are state-owned and the beer is produced by a state-owned brewery.

We investigated one or two inns to find out how this has affected matters. We were surprised to find that the beer was not at all bad and that unlike most government businesses this one was not only competing successfully with private enter-prise but was actually showing a profit. The beer was a penny less than most per pint and was quite drinkable. For all that there was a noticeable lack of interest and real concern for the customer in these state-owned inns, due to the lack of a land-lord with a financial stake in the takings. The managers were merely state employees and the result was a distinctly different atmosphere, efficient enough perhaps in a slipshod way, but not really welcoming or conducive to comfort.

Driving in search of Hadrian's Wall we came to Brampton, which is a strange mixture of new paint and dilapidation. It is an old town and, under the neglect and the modern additions, still an attractive one. This is an area where a depression set in when the Coal Board closed the numerous small pits here-abouts as uneconomic, but it now appears to be recovering.

We examined the old octagonal market house, now used as a bus shelter. Below were the solid metal stocks, now welded permanently shut. Beside them stood a policeman, who seemed uncertain whether we had designs on the local bank or were harmless visitors. We asked him if there was much crime in Brampton and, rather reluctantly, he confessed that there was not. He then pointed out the house where Prince Charles stayed during the '45, now a shoe shop, but proudly labelled. As it is outside the state-owned area, we investigated one or two inns. Each seemed to have 'taped' versions of that northern favourite, *The Blaydon Races*, playing loudly, but little spontaneous gaiety. The Cumbrians, like the Scots, tend to take their pleasures seriously.

The next stop on our route was Naworth Castle, for long the seat of the Dacres, wardens of the West March. Originally built in 1335, it was greatly added to in the sixteenth century by that Thomas Dacre prominent at Flodden and afterwards. At the end of the sixteenth century it passed by marriage of the heiress Elizabeth Dacre, known because of her estates as "Bessie of the Braid Apron", to the Howards. Her husband, Lord William Howard, better known as "Belted Will", was appointed by James I in 1606 to secure his "middle kingdom". He was a scholar and a writer and turned Naworth into a splendid Jacobean mansion house. His grandson assisted Charles II to regain his throne and was made 1st Earl of Carlisle. The castle, though severely damaged by fire in the nineteenth century, was skilfully restored and is still owned by the Carlisles.

Our guide book informed us that it was only open to the public on Thursdays between ten and five. We arrived rather guiltily at two minutes to five, hoping we would not find some irate custodian watch in hand standing by to bar the gates. However, there seemed to be no one about at all.

We were standing in the courtyard when an attractive feminine voice behind us enquired rather frostily:

"Is there anything you want?"

Turning round, we encountered the slightly indignant gaze of a lady in tweeds, who looked as if she must be the owner. We apologised for our lateness and explained that we had come to see over the castle. We were politely told that it was no longer open to the public and only then realised that our guide book was dated the previous year. Our apologies were gracefully accepted and we were invited to come in and look at the Great Hall, for it transpired, as we had already suspected, that our involuntary hostess was Lady Carlisle.

The Great Hall, large enough to take a full-sized badminton court, with a good deal to spare at each end, is hung with fine early Flemish tapestries. Prominent round the walls are four six-foot carved heraldic beasts mounted on plinths and holding banners. Just inside the main door is a handsome fish (see pl. 35), standing on his tail with a coronet on his head.

"You may recognise the Greystoke Fish?" Lady Carlisle suggested.

"I've a feeling we've met before somewhere," I admitted.

"He was the original for Tenniel's illustrations for *Alice in Wonderland*," explained Lady Carlisle. "And this, of course, is the Red Bull of Dacre."

She indicated a handsome red bull (see pl. 34) on one side of the cavernous fireplace.

"Ah, yes. The one who was on the wrong side at Flodden," I acknowledged.

It is planned to demolish the nineteenth-century block which was added when the castle was restored after the fire. Lady Carlisle made it plain that she and her husband intend to make it into a home to live in rather than a museum, which is as it should be, for it is preferable that such houses should be kept alive, changing slightly with the imprint of each age rather than remain a lifeless presentation of the past. At her suggestion we walked round the outside. It is splendidly placed on a bluff above the river Irthing with wonderful views across to the hills of Dumfriesshire and surrounded by gloriously wooded park land.

After this unintentional gate-crashing we drove down the hill to Lanercost. At the foot of the hill we passed a notable narrow old pack-horse bridge across the Irthing, now, perhaps fortunately, by-passed for modern traffic. Not far beyond lies the red brick sleeping ruin of Lanercost Priory.

Founded in 1166 by Sir Robert de Vaux, in memory of his father Sir Hubert de Vaux, many stones from the nearby Roman Wall were used in building this Augustinian Priory.

Due to its exposed position close to the Borders it must have suffered greatly from incessant Scottish raiding, but very little of its history is known. The oldest grave recorded there is that of Sir Rowland de Vaux, nephew of Robert, the founder. If these Vauxs were the ancestors of the family of brewers of that name, as seems most likely, then at least the brewhouse at Lanercost can claim to have originated one of the principal Border beers, in spite of governmental competition.

After the Dissolution of the Monasteries, the priory came into the hands of the Dacres, who converted part into a private dwelling house, while the rest was either quarried or allowed to decay. This process was probably accelerated when the junior branch of the family who lived there died out in the early eighteenth century. About this time the nave was converted into a parish church which still stands today.

Although unbalanced, like most such partial restorations, the church is quite impressive and there are some interesting old tombs behind it in the ruins. Most worth seeing to my mind, however, was the Dacre Hall, which is now Lanercost Village Hall. Few Senior Common Rooms amongst the colleges of Oxford and Cambridge could compare with the splendid proportions of this room. It must certainly be one of the finest village halls in the country.

Leaving Lanercost we continued eastward towards Hadrian's Wall. The first really fine example of it that we encountered was a good deal further on at Birdoswald. Here is a farmhouse and farmstead, part of which is actually built into the wall and all of which, with enormously thick walls, was clearly built centuries ago with stones from the wall. Beyond the farmhouse are the remains of a fort and to the east a length of the wall undulates over the ground and out of sight into a valley. Here for the first time one encounters the Roman presence in Britain with a sense of disbelief. It is such a solid piece of work still.

Looking northward we noticed several monstrous erections against the skyline. Studying them through binoculars, we came to the conclusion they could be nothing other than rockets. We decided to investigate them closer and drove to Spadeadam farm which seemed the most likely approach on the map. There was a fine fighting cock strutting proudly round the yard but no one at home. We withdrew to Gilsland and found a signpost "To Spadeadam Rocket Establishment". Beside it was another which read incongruously: "To Moscow ½ mile". Further on a larger notice read more intimidatingly: "No unauthorised person allowed beyond this point. By Order. Air Ministry Property."

This time I required no urging from my companion. I wrote and requested to be shown round. Somewhat to my surprise, I promptly received an invitation on Rolls Royce notepaper to visit them. Subsequently I discovered that Rolls Royce represented the Air Ministry in this case for there were four main firms involved, De Havilland Propellors Ltd., De Havilland Aircraft Ltd., Sperry Gyroscopes Co. Ltd., and over all Rolls Royce Ltd. This was in fact the home of Blue Streak, the only British rocket so far produced in the space age. Whatever else might be the case it represents a major triumph of co-ordination organised originally by the Ministry of Supply and passed on to the Ministry of Aircraft.

In 1956 it was decided to build a British Rocket Testing centre similar to Cape Canaveral (now Cape Kennedy) except that the firings would be static. The effect would be similar in every way to an actual launching except that the rocket would remain on the site. The problems were enormous. Not least the choice of a site. While it had to be isolated, it had also to be within reasonable range of population centres to supply labour. Spadeadam was chosen.

In three years over £20,000,000 was spent on the waste of bog and heather which had been part of the Earl of Carlisle's shooting (see pl. 36). Three main areas were established. An administrative area, with administrative offices, engine workshops, photographic laboratory, hospital and fire station. There also had to be a separate engine test area and thirdly, and most isolated, the rocket test area. All this involved a site eighteen miles in circumference bounded in the north by the State forest of Kielder. To add to the difficulties, much of the initial construction had to be in 'clean' conditions, as with the erection of the atomic plant at Chapelcross, since even a speck of dirt might cause an explosion.

Roads had to be laid over forty feet of liquid mud. Rocket servicing towers weighing 500 tons and some 110 feet high had to be built to run on rails on a 250-foot-long concrete test platform. Under the rocket test stand there had to be enormous steel flame deflectors to absorb and deflect the rocket engine blast into a concrete runway leading away from the platform.

Facing each of these huge launching test platforms, and there are two, they sited an underground control chamber with periscope, viewing mirrors, enclosed TV circuit for viewing details of the rocket and all the controls for each aspect of the rocket's launching. Thus the entire programme of a launching could be simulated and every aspect tested without the rocket leaving the ground.

Enormous quantities of water, electricity and fuel are required. Water is used to cool the flame as the rocket is fired and ten million gallons a week were calculated as likely to be needed. Most is extracted from the river Irthing and diverted to a settling lake after use, where the effluent is removed, after which it is returned to storage tanks and re-used. Electricity comes from the National Grid near Carlisle and since this, in turn, is supplied in part by Chapelcross it can be said that atomic power plays its part. On the site there are over twenty miles of overhead wires and well over a thousand miles of internal wiring.

The fuels used are liquid oxygen and kerosene under pressure from gaseous nitrogen. Each rocket contains 60 tons of liquid oxygen and 26 tons of kerosene. If these mix accidentally the explosive potential is equivalent per ton to 10 tons of

& 33. "The enormous bulk of the nuclear power station at Chapelcross (*above*) minates the scene (p. 168). Peel towers (like this one *below* at Torthorwald, 162) were the natural products of their age: it now seems we are contemplating th equanimity leaving our own larger and dangerously radioactive eyesores behind us."

"The Red Bull of Deese and the Graystoke Fish, the original for Tenniel's illustrations for *Alice in Wonderland*."

TNT, hence the need for an isolated site, even though the rockets do not leave the ground. The rockets themselves are 60 feet long and 10 feet round with a metal skin 500th of an inch thick, so that when not in use they have to be kept inflated with helium gas to prevent them buckling.

The rockets are driven by two Rolls Royce engines mounted on gymbals which are controlled to provide the angle of thrust and thus the direction. By 'gymballing' the rocket engines on the test pad when firing, precise calculations can be made as to the estimated flight and conditions throughout can be carefully studied. Films taken automatically by cameras mounted at critical points throughout each simulated launching are played back afterwards and examined minutely. It can therefore be readily appreciated that each such test firing represents considerable expenditure in terms of fuel, money and effort.

My companion and I knew nothing of all this when we presented ourselves at the gates by appointment.

CHAPTER 10

Spadeadam to Berwick

To the hunting, ho! cried Parcy Reed,
The morning sun is on the dew;
The cauler breeze frae off the fells,
Will lead the dogs to the quarry true.

"THE DEATH OF PARCY REED"

OUR ARRIVAL at the Rocket Establishment was expected. We were presented with a pass and directed to the administrative block. From thereon everything ran smoothly and efficiently as might be expected of an establishment run by Rolls Royce. We were duly conducted round the entire place.

On leaving the administrative area we were asked to wear plastic safety helmets. Examining these light and neat plastic helmets I noted they were made in West Germany. My companion complained that his gave him a headache after a few minutes' wear, but I did not personally find mine at all uncomfortable.

It was explained that the testing site is identical to the firing range at Woomera so that the rockets and crews may be tested here together before going out to Australia for actual launching. In the underground control chamber we were introduced to an amiable young giant, who was the 'boffin' in charge. He started with quiet satisfaction to explain the serried banks of control dials in a pleasant Yorkshire accent. Within a few minutes my mind was reeling under the impact of scientific data. To appreciate why, it is only necessary to mention that there are over 8 million yards of wire involved. Eventually in a spirit of pure gamesmanship I interrupted the steady flow of information:

"Where does the electricity for all this come from?"

"Electricity?" he queried blankly.

"Power," I corrected myself.

"I don't know," he admitted, with a shrug.

It was obviously a question which had never even occurred to him. To him, like most people, water comes out of a tap and electricity, or power, down a wire. It was an endearingly human trait to uncover, even if he obviously considered anyone who could ask such a question as beyond the pale. It also showed the degree of specialisation involved. He was not concerned with administration. His job was rocket launching and he was obviously supremely competent at that. Here indeed was the space age engine driver, hero of every space-minded schoolboy.

We watched a test firing. It was due to last 106 seconds, but was cut short impressively after two and a half. As we were the nearest people above ground, in a special observer's post three-quarters of a mile from the test site, I was glad all went well with the emergency cut-out switch. The powerful roar and thick half-mile cloud produced by the exhaust even during that short time, as well as the tension noticeable amongst the watchers, was still impressive enough for me.

It was all extraordinarily interesting. I had not expected to be fascinated, but I was. Here was the test bench of the future. In this sort of crucible the fate of the world was being obscured by clouds of exhaust gases. It was a sobering thought.

It is impossible not to feel sorry for the group of men involved in this venture. Politics have bedevilled the issue. In 1960, after only eighteen months' experiment, further work on Blue Streak was suspended. After a year in limbo the European Space Launcher Development Organisation, E.L.D.O., was formed, which resulted in a reprieve. On the lines of a mixed-manned fleet and likely to be as effective, this plans to use Blue

Streak as the base with a French booster rocket above it, a secondary West German booster rocket above that and an Italian satellite on top of the lot.

While it may have been right to discontinue work on Blue Streak as a weapon, we do now have the exciting possibility of using it for peaceful scientific purposes. These men at Spadeadam are efficient. They have already produced improvements on the original launching pad designs. There has already been an impressive demonstration of what can be achieved in a short time. Given time and backing we could certainly produce our own booster rockets and satellites. The amount of money involved is not great compared with the future possible gains. At the very lowest level, this investment has already brought increasing prosperity to a depressed area in Cumberland, where over 2,000 are now employed. Given wholehearted support, the future possibilities are endless. Ours might be only a tiny effort compared with those of the U.S.A. and the U.S.S.R., but that is where future development lies and the key is there at Spadeadam.

We drove away from there through the small village of Gilsland in a thoughtful mood. My companion summed it up nicely:

"Most of what I saw there was miles above my head, but as that's the ultimate destination anyway, perhaps that's just as it should be."

We went in search of Hadrian's Wall. The stretch at Birdoswald, though well preserved, lies in a peaceful wooded valley. By Walltown Crags the wildness of the countryside is more impressive (see pl. 37). From here onwards the Great Whin Sill, that strange geological formation, which ends in the sea at the Farne Islands beyond Bamburgh, projects its rocky escarpments above ground for many miles. It is a country of changing moods and changing colours, of dark moorland, craggy hillsides and windswept desolation. Seen in a misty dawn, with white tendrils blotting out the chill grey landscape, yesterday's sunlight is easily forgotten. It requires no great imagination then to picture this countryside as it was in Roman times, a boggy, unwelcoming, stony wilderness.

The Wall stretches 73½ miles from Wallsend-on-Tyne to the Solway. It was started on Hadrian's arrival in Britain about A.D. 122 and finished within ten years. A good deal about it must still remain conjecture, but it seems probable that an extensive ditch and earthwork was first built, known as the Vallum and still visible some distance south of the Wall itself. There were at this time three Legions in Britain, amounting to about 8,000 men, and each Century (100 men) built a stretch of fifty yards at a time.

There is a splendid Roman regularity about it. There were some fifteen forts along it, varying in size mostly from three to five acres. These held, according to size, either 500 or 1,000 infantry, or 500 cavalry. Between each were mile castles spaced at intervals of one Roman mile, 1,620 yards, garrisoned with forty men. Between each mile castle two four-men turrets divided the wall into three equal lengths. A message could thus easily be passed the entire length by word of mouth.

The width of the Wall was 7 feet 6 inches and the height has been estimated at about 15 feet with a further 5-foot parapet to the north. Today no section remains anything like entire, or much more than 6 feet high, so extensively has it been quarried over the ages. It is still, to my mind, the most impressive of Roman remains in this country.

We investigated another stretch beyond Walltown. Sheep were grazing all round it, and even on it, but it seemed to be in a remarkable state of preservation. Following it further along I discovered to my surprise that it was being systematically dismantled stone by stone and rebuilt with concrete by a Ministry of Works team. It rather spoiled my visions of a wall erected by nameless legionaries in A.D. 122 to realise that it had been taken down and rebuilt by nameless Ministry of Works labourers in the 1960s.

"This is obviously the Government's answer to all those 'English Go Home' signs you Scots have been putting up," laughed my friend. "They're rebuilding Hadrian's Wall, but they're keeping quiet about it."

It should of course be realised that the Wall was never intended as a purely defensive measure. The forts were mostly sited in the Wall and their main gate faced north so that the troops could sally out to deal with any disturbances reported nearby. The foundations of perhaps the most impressively sited fort are at Housesteads, a short if steep climb from the road, where well-preserved sections of the Wall are also to be seen to the west. Further east is the cavalry fort of Chesters, also of some interest with the foundations of the bath house and a vaulted strongroom still visible.

Long before the discovery of this vaulted strongroom, there was an old local legend that on certain moonlit nights 500 ghostly horsemen might be seen emerging from underground stables at Chesters to scour the neighbouring countryside. It was there that the 2nd Asturian, or Spanish, cavalry were stationed, 500 strong. It seems strange that this belief should perpetuate the exact number of horsemen and it is difficult to avoid linking this with the ghostly legion of Bowden Moor.

The comparatively recent growth of interest in archaeology is underlined by the fact that none of these remains were seriously investigated until John Clayton, Town Clerk of Newcastle, who died in 1890, started excavating around 1840, after inheriting the estate of Chesters from his father. Prior to that there is scarcely any reference to the ruins. Although their preservation and that of long stretches of the Wall is almost entirely due to John Clayton even his methods of excavation and records were haphazard by present-day standards. It is only on visiting Hexham that one realises how persistently the Wall must have been quarried over the centuries.

Here is perhaps the most mediaeval of all the Border towns. A most attractive small market town, it is overladen with antiquity. With its magnificent Abbey Church, its Moot Hall and its pillared market place it is historic enough. When one appreciates that most of these were built in turn with Roman stones taken from the Wall, and from the forts at Chesters and nearby Corstopitum, it becomes an antiquarian's delight.

The glory of Hexham undoubtedly is its Abbey Church. Though much restored, it is as fine as many cathedrals and a good deal larger than some. Originally a church was built here in A.D. 674 by Wilfrid of Ripon, but this was destroyed by Danish invaders in the ninth century and only the crypt remains —which in itself is a fascinating spectacle with Roman stones prominent in its walls (see pl. 38). The present church was built in the twelfth century, but the nave and the east end of the chancel were destroyed by the Scots in the thirteenth century. The east end was rebuilt in 1858 and the nave in 1908. From the north side the exterior has a noticeable resemblance to Jedburgh.

The effect inside of an intermingling of Roman, Saxon and mediaeval relics against a background, in places, of obviously fresh stonework is most extraordinary. Here is the monument to a young Roman cavalryman beside a mediaeval stair. A carving depicts him with his lance about to ride down a kneeling warrior, which incidentally shows that the Britons used the same tactics against cavalry in those days as the Sudanese in the nineteenth century, kneeling to the charge and hamstringing the horses as they passed.

The inscription, translated, reads:

"To the Gods, the Shades. Flavinus of the Cavalry Regiment of Petriana, a Standard Bearer of the White Troop. Aged 25 and of seven years service is buried here."

Among the remarkable Saxon relics is a unique tiny silver chalice, a stone font on a Roman base and the Frith Stool, a solid stone chair, accepted as having been the bishop's seat and a place of sanctuary in mediaeval days. To do justice to the Roman and mediaeval carvings or the remarkable triptychs dating from the fifteenth century it is necessary to visit the church to study them personally. It must suffice to say that here was an abbey church in the Borders which survived without being totally destroyed. Viewing it, one realises more clearly than ever what a loss was suffered by the destruction of the others.

While in the neighbourhood of Hexham, it is well worth crossing the Tyne and visiting the Roman camp and museum of Corstopitum, above Corbridge. From there a quick circular tour can be made to the hidden village of Blanchland, which was once all part of another twelfth-century abbey, reputedly betrayed by its bells and destroyed by the raiding Scots in the thirteenth century. The return to Hexham is over real Borders country, wild moorland now much afforested.

Just short of Chollerton, I realised that this must be the point referred to in the ballad of *Jock o' the Side* where they had rescued Jock most audaciously from Newcastle prison and galloped off, chains and all:

> Oh Jock! sae winsomely ye sit,
>   Wi' baith yer feet upon ae side;
> Sae weel ye're harneist and sae trig,
>   In troth ye sit like ony bride.
>
> The night, tho' wat, they did na mind,
>   But hied them on fu' merrilie,
> Until they cam to Cholerton brae,
>   Where the water ran like mountains hie.

All the same, they crossed the North Tyne safely and joked at the expense of their pursuers once they were safely on the other side heading for Liddesdale again. Not so happy was Archie Armstrong of Liddesdale, left in the dungeon of nearby Haughton Castle by Sir Thomas Swinburne, who journeyed to York before remembering his prisoner. He hurried back to find, like the Jardine laird in similar circumstances, that his victim had gnawed his own flesh from his bones in agonies of hunger and thirst.

From the high ground a little further on, the view to the west across the valley of the North Tyne is very fine. The line of Hadrian's Wall is distinctly visible on the escarpments of the Great Whin Sill and, though the wild rolling moors beyond give way eventually to the darker line of the State forest of Kielder, there is still a strong impression that this is a frontier region, wild and untamed. We paused for a short while to admire it.

"You know," remarked my friend, "I don't in the least mind millions being spent at Spadeadam, but I do grudge the thousands that must have been expended rebuilding Hadrian's Wall simply to turn this island into an olde worlde tourist trap."

"It's fairly obvious, from all we've seen," I retorted, "that practically no one anywhere on the Borders is seriously interested in tourists, so you don't need to worry unduly."

We drove onwards, passing over the hump-backed bridge and beside the park of the seventeenth-century Wallington Hall, well placed above the Wansbeck valley, with three boulder-sized gargoyle heads facing the road above the ha-ha. Home of the late Sir G. M. Trevelyan, the famous historian, it is now owned by the National Trust. Originally built in 1688, it was enlarged in 1740 and in 1855 Ruskin designed the central hall.

Here we turned aside to Morpeth, taking the road through the rather attractive countryside around Mitford. Morpeth is a surprisingly pleasant old town, in spite of the constant rumble of heavy traffic and in spite of the plans to double the population by a further ten thousand. Its old main street is one of the many bottlenecks in the Great North Road beyond Newcastle. Prominent beside it is the gateway tower supposedly built by William, Baron Greystock, in the fourteenth century and still standing. Once the seat of the Dacres, the town has strong associations with the Earl of Carlisle, whose eldest son takes the title of Viscount Morpeth.

By appointment we went to meet the mayor, Mr. W. Sanderson, a well-known and well-beloved elder of the town, now in his eighties but still as jaunty as ever. It has been his habit since the Boer war to wear a ten-gallon hat and this particular trait has been the subject of an article or two in the *Hatter's Gazette*. So well known is this particular characteristic that he has even received free hats from various parts of the world. With such a colourful character a great many stories are current about him, all of which he enjoys recounting with gusto.

When first mayor and thus automatically chairman of the bench of magistrates he was still connected with Vaux, concerned chiefly with buying their new properties. It was second nature with him always to stand drinks all round whenever visiting an inn. Entering a local inn on one occasion he duly ordered drinks for everyone present. Informed that there were two ladies in the Bottle and Jug, discreetly partitioned off from the main bar, he expansively included them in the order. The sequel came the next morning when an elderly female harridan was brought before the bench, accused of being drunk and disorderly.

"How could that be?" she demanded shrilly, "when I was drinking with his worship the Mayor himself?"

We drove past the old gateway tower and crossed the river Wansbeck beyond it to visit the new housing development at the top of the hill beyond. It was by no means completed but we became hopelessly lost amongst the unfinished roads and buildings. After passing the same plastic flamingo for the fourth or fifth time we stopped in desperation and asked for help from a young couple. To judge by the numbers of young children playing thereabouts it is mostly populated by similar young married couples and their families, quite capable of doubling the population yet again.

From Morpeth we made a cross-country journey through most attractive Northumbrian country to a field trial on the Simonside Moors south of Rothbury. The sign of the curlew by the roadside showed us that again we had entered the national park. The field trial was being organised by a sporting young farmer named Sanderson and, struck by the coincidence, I started to tell him about the mayor. I really ought to have known better.

"You don't want to believe all the stories you hear about my grandfather," he remarked, with a twinkle in his eye reminiscent of his grandsire.

It was a field trial for pointer-retrievers, but unfortunately the weather had been so bad in the previous weeks, with continuous rain and high winds, that the birds rose very wild. It must have been extremely difficult to judge in the circumstances, but it was a very pleasant day to be a spectator. The views from these moors are extremely extensive, over to the Cheviots on one side and to the coast on the other.

We continued on through Rothbury on to the moorland road to Alnwick, which has wonderful views of the changing Northumbrian scene. The first part is over moorland, but beyond that one sees the fertile valleys between the Cheviots and the coastal belt. It was as we crossed the main Morpeth to Wooler road surrounded by bare moorland that my companion voiced his thoughts.

"You know," he said, "looking at Spadeadam just showed what can be done when people set their minds to it. Here's the sort of place to build a new town. Right slap bang in the middle of nowhere, instead of doubling the size of a place like Morpeth, which merely means making it a suburb of Newcastle and increasing its urban sprawl."

"As a dual-carriageway is being built in the west it must eventually be balanced by a similar road in the east," I pointed out. "In that case you will inevitably find a town like Alnwick doubling itself in size, anyway, as new industries gravitate there. If the pledges to open up the north-east mean anything, that must happen."

"Maybe, but in how many years' time?" asked my friend.

As we drove down the final steep hill into Alnwick I could not help wondering what the answer to that question was. For Alnwick, along with Hexham, has claims to being the most mediaeval of the Border towns. It is a grey and gated old market town, with a cobbled market place and narrow winding mediaeval streets, but it is still dominated by the protective battlements of the ducal castle on the northern outskirts, standing strategically above a steep descent to the river Aln. Tucked in a hollow beside the castle, Alnwick no longer conveys an embattled readiness to stand to arms against raiders from over the Cheviots. It has a sleepy air as of an elderly warrior who has laid aside his sword and is content to sit by the fireside.

It is perhaps characteristic of Alnwick that one of its principal industries, for which it has world-wide fame, is the manufacture of fishing rods. At the opposite end of the town to the castle, outside the confines of the Hotspur Gate, stands Hardy's factory. For over ninety years and for four generations of the same family Hardy's of Alnwick have been manufacturing fishing rods. In the fascinating old-fashioned factory, built in the best Victorian traditions, elderly craftsmen who have been with the firm all their lives continue to practise their acquired skills in rod-making. The whole building is permeated with the fine bamboo sawdust and each man, as a matter of course, is a keen fisherman.

It is an education to watch each stage of a rod's development and to witness the care that goes into it. The precision engineering required for modern reel-making is astonishing. This side of the industry is not so evident in the much smaller rival second generation breakaway firm of Walker Bampton just round the corner. Here too, however, on a smaller scale, one sees the same dedication to a craft. Here too, one can see girls, skilled workers every one, busy with nimble fingers turning out the gaily coloured trout and salmon flies, which in due course may grace the fishing book, or hat, of some ardent fisherman, or possibly even one day catch a fish.

A pointer to the future may lie in the fact that Hardy's are planning to move into a larger, more modern factory sited close to the by-pass which is being built round the town. At present all the heavy traffic on the Great North Road must patiently wend its way through the winding main streets of the old town before coming to the steep descent to the River Aln. Since the bridge, decorated with the lion of the Percies, is only wide enough for one lorry at a time, a bottleneck can easily form here. As yet, however, plans are only being made for a two-lane by-pass round the town, not for a dual-carriageway from Newcastle onwards. This is hardly likely to bring fresh life to the town. At present Alnwick belongs in the stagecoach age and appears satisfied that this should be so. For the visitor it has considerable charm.

The castle is undoubtedly the focal point in Alnwick. Here is the seat of the Percies. To the Scots Borderer Alnwick and Naworth must always be two of the most interesting castles on the English side if only for their connection with the memorable names of Percy and Dacre. So much Border history is contained in names alone. Percy and Northumberland, Douglas and Buccleuch, Dacre and Ker, sound like a peal of war trumpets down the ages.

It is all the more surprising therefore to find that Alnwick was not originally connected with the name Percy. When the castle was originally built has now been long lost in the mists of time. The first mention of it is in the ownership of Baron Yvo de Vesci in 1096. The de Vescis died out at the turn of the thirteenth century and in 1309 the castle was bought by Sir Henry de Percy. It was his great-grandson who became 1st Earl of Northumberland; and his son in turn was the Hotspur immortalised somewhat inaccurately by Shakespeare in *Henry IV*—for though Hotspur was killed at Shrewsbury in 1403 there was no suggestion that he was killed by Henry. The 2nd earl's cousin, killed in 1436 in a battle with the Douglases, was probably the Percy of *Chevy Chase*.

On the whole, the Percies seem to have been an ill-fated lot. They either seem to have conspired to rebel at the wrong moment, or to have loyally backed the wrong side. Thus the 6th earl was misguided enough to love Anne Boleyn before Henry VIII. Though he saved his neck, his brothers, both staunch Catholics, were executed and he died in poverty. The 7th earl, his nephew, who ultimately succeeded under Mary, was beheaded as a staunch Roman Catholic by Elizabeth. The 8th earl was arrested on suspicion of Catholicism and died mysteriously in the Tower.

In 1670, with the death of the 11th earl, the earldom lapsed. Succession continued through the female line. Sir Hugh Smithson, a Yorkshire baronet, married the heiress and succeeded to the estates and earldom in 1750, taking the surname of Percy. In 1766 he was created 1st Duke of Northumberland by George III.

It was around 1755 that the 1st Duke started restoring the castle, which by this time had fallen into almost complete ruin through the various vicissitudes of the centuries, the previous Percies having preferred Warkworth. The Duke employed Robert Adam as his architect and the entire castle was rebuilt, on the original Norman foundations, in 'Strawberry Hill' Gothic. This was, however, almost entirely altered again under the 4th duke in 1854 in an ambitious restoration, which was not completed at his death in 1865. He employed the foremost Italian architects to remodel the interior on Renaissance lines. Only a few further alterations were made by the 7th duke early in the present century.

The effect, therefore, today is that the castle, though built on Norman foundations and outwardly mediaeval, is almost entirely a product of the nineteenth century. This does not make it any the less interesting. The interior, indeed, is somewhat staggering, as if one had wandered into a Florentine palace. It is certainly magnificent in the true sense of the word. Astonishingly enough, it does not give the impression of merely being a showpiece, or a museum, but has a genuinely lived-in atmosphere.

We did not spend very long in the castle, but as we had permission to visit the grounds we turned in that direction. On the way out we stopped to glance at the ducal stables. The Duke is, of course, M.F.H. of the Percy and a keen huntsman. Unfortunately, the horses were out, but I was delighted to see that the handsome wooden ducal horse buckets in front of each box are painted light blue and have a gold coronet on them. The Duke has a covered riding school close behind the stables, which must be particularly useful in hard weather. It is the only ducal indoor manège in the Borders.

We went to look at Hulne Priory. Little of this is left except an impressively thick outer wall and some grass-grown ruins inside. Amongst these is the weather-worn statue of a monk at his prayers in which the sculptor has skilfully implanted a sense of urgency that is still powerfully apparent. It appears that the 1st duke thought he might 'improve' these ruins, but the result merely seems to have confused all traces of the original.

The grounds are themselves worth the visit simply for their very considerable beauty. Close to the priory is what looked like the head keeper's house, to judge by the pheasant coops close to it. Looking at the valley below one could visualise some splendid shooting of tremendously high birds over guns stationed there. The rolling moorland outside the walls looked like excellent hunting country as well, so that the Duke has the best of both sporting worlds, quite apart from some likely looking fishing in the Aln.

The present (10th) Duke of Northumberland married Lady Elizabeth Montague Douglas Scott, daughter of the present Duke of Buccleuch, thus finally ending the old rivalry of Percy and Douglas and uniting the two chief ducal houses on each side of the Borders. In the entire Borders area there are no larger private landowners than the Dukes of Northumberland and Buccleuch. Yet, though the Percy holdings probably amount to around 100,000 acres in Northumberland, they are small beside the Buccleuch Estate holdings on the other side of the Border. In each case, however, it must be remembered that a very considerable proportion of the land in question is moor, hill, or forest land, fit only for trees or sheep pasture at best. In comparison with the maps of their respective counties these apparently large holdings are seen in perspective.

There are, perhaps, differences in their generations noticeable between the two dukes. Alnwick Castle is opened to the public, Drumlanrig and Bowhill are not. It is plain indeed that the Duke of Buccleuch shuns any form of publicity and prefers to lead as private a life as possible consistent with his public duties. In view of the antics of certain dukes today who can blame him.

Yet there are considerable parallels between these two large ducal landowners. Both live on their estates and take a direct interest in running them. Although amongst the largest estates in the country, there is little question that both are extremely well run. It may be argued that there is an element of feudalism in the ownership and management of such large blocks of land by private individuals, whether dukes or commoners. The fact remains that unless any estate is run efficiently today it very quickly goes to the wall, regardless of size or who owns it.

Without particular reference to these estates, there are certain trends noticeable in farming throughout the country today, which perhaps apply with particular force in the Borders. Although on average the ordinary sheep farm is an economic unit the same cannot be said of the smaller arable farms. The tendency throughout the country is the consolidation of several such small farms wherever possible into one larger unit. The result is a slow depopulation of the countryside similar to that mentioned in the *Statistical Account* in the eighteenth century. Increasing mechanisation on the farms is adding to this tendency everywhere.

The drift is still away to the larger towns. Agricultural areas

5 & 37. "Spadeadam Rocket Establishment. The home of Blue Streak, the only ritish rocket produced in this space age" (p. 179). Within sight of Hadrian's 'all at Walltown, "still the most impressive of Roman remains in this country." (p. 185)

38. "The monument to a young Roman cavalryman," Hexham Abbey (p. 187

such as the Borders, particularly perhaps the northern part of Northumberland, are extremely sparsely populated by contrast. To some extent this can be related to the standard of the roads throughout the Borders. Though in good condition, they are mainly secondary class and winding. They were built for horses and not for cars. Until they are improved it will be difficult to attract industry and the steady depopulation will continue.

Although the Borders are unlikely to be opened up to industry on any scale without dual-carriageways there are already signs of another change taking place. The pressure of population and the number of cars in the south is now so great that they must find space regardless of the state of the roads. It appears that increasingly the Borders are becoming the playground of the industrial half of the country.

Inevitably, whether the Borderer likes it or not, the Borders seem destined for tourism. At present there is only a lukewarm interest in the idea and the area is scarcely known or publicised. Yet the Borders have a tremendous amount to offer, not least almost empty roads off the beaten track. Though there are few really first-rate hotels there are equally few really bad ones. Almost anywhere in the Borders fishing can be had in season, though shooting is harder to obtain. Pony trekking has been started in places and golf is obtainable almost everywhere. For the hardy the sea bathing on the north-east coast is splendid, with miles of uncrowded sandy beaches.

It is only fair to add one word of caution. A guide to Northumberland in the eighteenth century noted:

A county of a sharp and piercing air and much troubled with pinching frosts, boisterous winds and deep snows in the winter, which would be more offensive to its inhabitants were it not for the great plenty of sea coal here had at such easie rates.

We continued on the road towards Wooler, turning off to Chillingham. The well-known herd of wild white cattle there are reputed to be the direct and pure-bred descendants of some

o

197

original wild cattle walled in when the land was emparked in the thirteenth century. Although Pennant described the cattle he saw at Drumlanrig in 1772 at some length, as we have noted, on his return from the north later in his tour he merely recorded at Chillingham: "In the park are between thirty and forty cattle, of the same kind with those described at Drumlanrig."

In Thomas Bewick's *History of Quadrupeds* written in 1790 is the following description of the Chillingham herd, supplied "by a former bailiff of the Earl of Tankerville".

Their colour is invariably white, muzzle black; the whole of the inside of the ear, and about one-third of the outside from the tip downwards red; horns white, with black tips very fine, and bent upwards. Some of the bulls have a thin upright mane, about an inch and a half or two inches long . . . At the first appearance of any person they set off at full speed and gallop to a considerable distance, when they wheel round and come boldly up again, tossing their heads in a menacing manner . . . This they do several times, shortening their distance and advancing nearer, till they come within a few yards, when most people think it prudent to leave them . . .

Although published in 1790 there is no saying when a "former bailiff" had been employed at Chillingham. It might have been ten or even twenty years earlier. The point is that Pennant's description of the herd at Drumlanrig tallies with the Chillingham herd as it is today as well, if not better, than Bewick's secondhand description. Add to this the report that the Chillingham herd was reduced to one cow and calf in 1760 and it seems improbable to say the least that there were 30–40 in 1772, especially as they are not notably reliable breeders, unless some outside source had replenished their numbers.

Suspicion hardens to certainty on reading a note by Dr. Ramage written in 1876 about the Drumlanrig herd: "There is a tradition that about one hundred years ago the whole stock was sold and driven off to Chillingham." 'Old Q' was intent on turning all his assets at Drumlanrig into cash, but it was unlikely that he simply had the herd butchered, and who more likely to buy them than the Earl of Tankerville to boost his ailing stock? That he appears to have been successful may be inferred from the fact that in the first decade of the nineteenth century the herd numbered 120.

When the transfer took place cannot be certain. Since 1790 onwards the successive earls of Tankerville have been extremely strict about keeping the stock pure, so that it is virtually certain that the Drumlanrig herd had been introduced before that date, even possibly during Pennant's absence in the north in 1772. Considering the stress subsequently laid on their purity of blood and ancient origins it is not surprising that on making an enquiry to the Chillingham agent in 1876, Dr. Ramage received the answer that there was no record of the transfer. The fact that they have undoubtedly been inbred for nearly two hundred years and do relate to the old wild white cattle is however surely impressive enough.

Bewick's description of the herd continued:

When the cows calve they hide their calves for a week or ten days in some sequestered situation and go and suckle them two or three times a day. If any person comes near the calves they clap their heads close to the ground and lie like a hare in form to hide themselves. This is a proof of their native wildness and is corroborated by the following circumstance that happened to the writer of this narrative, who found a hidden calf two months old, very lean and very weak. On stroking its head it got up, pawed two or three times like an old bull, bellowed very loud, retired a few paces and bolted at his legs with all its force. It then began to paw again, bellowed, stepped back and bolted as before; but knowing its intention and stepping aside, it missed him, fell, and was so very weak it could not rise, though it made several efforts. But it had done enough; the whole herd was alarmed and coming to its rescue obliged him to retire, for the dams will suffer no person to touch their calves without attacking them with impetuous ferocity. When any happens to be wounded or grown weak and feeble, through age or sickness, the rest of the herd set upon it and gore it to death.

Visiting the herd today is not the exciting experience it once seems to have been, but visitors must be accompanied by the keeper.

"We haven't lost any visitors yet," I heard him reassure a nervous enquirer.

It is a pleasant walk across the park and the cattle are interesting. They resemble distinctly the cave paintings of aurochs, with curving horns and small feet. Their continued survival is attributed to the fact that the strongest and fittest bull becomes 'King of the Herd'. During his reign he allows no other bulls to mate with the cows. He remains 'King' only as long as no other bull can successfully challenge him.

Apart from this and their high-pitched trumpeting bellow the three characteristics of most interest not already mentioned are, firstly, their apparent immunity to disease. They do not appear to suffer from any of the normal cattle ailments beyond persistent scouring, which does not seem to affect them. Secondly, although they have particularly thin skins they do not suffer from warble flies. Thirdly, their blood does not appear to belong to any of the normal categories of cattle blood groups. The difficulties in the way of any vet examining the cattle are, however, considerable since if they are handled by humans they are then gored to death by the rest of the herd. Thus they have to be on the point of death before a live blood sample can be taken.

Since the disastrous winter of 1947 when the herd was nearly wiped out they have been supported by voluntary subscription. Long gone are the days described by Bewick:

The mode of killing them was perhaps the only modern remains of the grandeur of ancient hunting. On notice being given that a wild bull would be killed upon a certain day, the inhabitants of the neighbourhood came in great numbers, both horse and foot. The horsemen rode off the bull from the rest of the herd, until he stood at bay, when a marksman dismounted and shot. At some of these huntings twenty or thirty shots have been fired before he was subdued. On such occasions the bleeding victim grew desperately furious from the smarting of his wounds and the shouts of savage joy that were echoing from every side. From the number of accidents that happened, this dangerous mode has been seldom practised of late years, the park keeper alone generally shooting them with a rifled gun at one shot.

In October 1872 the Prince of Wales shot the King of the herd, firing from a concealed position in a hay cart. This gave rise to a piece of Northumbrian satire, by a Mr. Robert Elliott:

> He's a warrier, ye knaa, and the papors are full
> Iv a tarrible encounter he had wiv a bull!
> He slowtered the bull, but his critics will say
> That the Prince was cuncealed in a bundle iv hay;
> An' thit it was ne feat at a' te lie hid
> An' slowter the bull in the way that he did;
> But some fokes are selfish an' winna hear tell
> Iv ony great feats unless dune be thorsel.

Before leaving Chillingham we took a look round the little church. It has a Norman doorway, but its particular pride must undoubtedly be the outstanding tomb of Sir Ralph Grey and his wife Lady Elizabeth Grey dating from the fifteenth century. Its elaborate carving and ornamentation survived the excesses of the Reformation and subsequent religious bigotry and are now suffering merely from the ravages of time and neglect.

We did not detour round by Wooler, which is a quiet little market town without a great deal to recommend it. We continued on instead, more or less directly towards Berwick, over the moors amid rather attractive scenery. At a bend in the road by Barmoor we came upon a War Memorial in the shape of a rough-hewn boulder by the roadside with the names of the dead carved on it. Its sheer simplicity commands attention and respect.

We struck the Great North Road once more a matter of three or four miles south of Berwick. It must have been around here towards the end of James II's reign that a mysterious high-wayman twice running held up the mail successfully. Amongst the alleged plotters against the king's life was one Sir John Cochrane, whose life was saved by this intercession, for on each occasion his death warrant had been amongst the mail and the delay gave his relations time to gain his reprieve. On his release Sir John himself was greeted by the masked figure, who turned out to be none other than his own daughter Grizel Cochrane.

From the top of the steep descent above Tweedmouth the red tiles and grey slates of Berwick can be seen on the other side of the Tweed. On the left is the Merse and the slopes of the Lammermoors, on the right is the sea and the rocky outline of the coast. The view is a good one, but it is a bad place to stop with a steady stream of heavy traffic toiling up the hill. We were nearly back at our starting point and, having begun there by quoting Dr. Fuller, it seems only fair to give him the last word. He recorded:

We cannot close our observations without adverting to that cruel and dangerous practice which carters in general have of over-driving their master's horses . . . Notwithstanding the various regulations that have hitherto been made for restraining drivers of carts from driving furiously . . . the object still remains unattained . . . scarcely a day passes but we hear of some accident happening from the carelessness of drivers and their generally driving too fast. Several lives have been lost in Berwick and its suburbs within these few years past from these causes.

Further Reading

A full bibliography on the Borders would be impossibly lengthy but I give here a few suggestions for any reader who would like them. Some of the books, including my own main sources, are rather old but could be obtained through a library; others are more recent.

Tours in Scotland by Thomas Pennant, 1769–1772.
A Sporting Tour of the Highlands and Great Part of the North of England by Colonel Thomas Thornton, 1784.
The First *Statistical Account of Scotland* is a twenty-one-volume compilation. In 1790, Sir John Sinclair, then a lay member of the General Assembly of the Kirk of Scotland, decided to gather together a single description of the whole of Scotland from material supplied by parish ministers. Each parish in Scotland has a section and though they vary in readability, the best of them are full of charm as well as of valuable information. The Second (written in the 1830's) and Third *Statistical Accounts* take the story on.
Tales of the Borders and of Scotland, a ten-volume collection by John Mackay Wilson.
History of North Durham by J. Raine.
History and Antiquities of Berwick-upon-Tweed including Tweedmouth, Spittal etc. by Dr. John Fuller, 1852.
A Thousand Miles of Wandering along the Roman Wall, the Old Border Region, Lakeland and Ribbesdale, by Edmund Bogg, 1898.
Highways and Byways of the Borders by Andrew and John Lang, 1913.
North and South of the Tweed by Jean Laing.
Drumlanrig and the Douglases.
A Short History of Scotland by P. Hume Brown (new ed. 1951, Oliver & Boyd).

Minstrelsy of the Scottish Border
Guy Mannering $\Big\}$ by Sir Walter Scott.
Redgauntlet

Sir Walter Scott by John Buchan, 1932.
Life of Scott by John Wilson Lockhart, 1838.
The Scott Originals by W. S. Crockett, 1912.

The Oxford Book of Ballads ed. J. Quiller Couch, O.U.P. (many editions).

The Poetical Works of James Hogg.

Index

205

INDEX

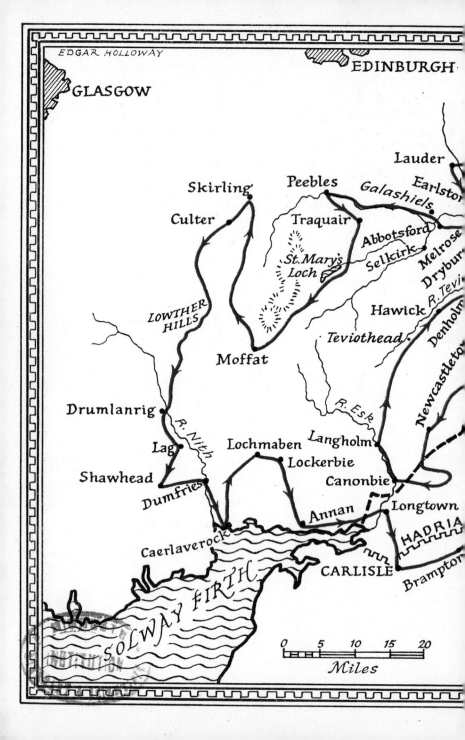